Motorbooks International Illustrated Buyer's Guide Series

Illustrated

FORD

Pickup

BUYER'S ★ GUIDE™

Paul G. McLaughlin

Motorbooks International
Publishers & Wholesalers

A heartfelt thank-you to Bernice, Paul, Amy and Jessica for their time, understanding and patience.

First published in 1991 by Motorbooks International Publishers & Wholesalers, P O Box 2, 729 Prospect Avenue, Osceola, WI 54020 USA

Motorbooks International books are also available at discounts in bulk quantity for industrial or sales-promotional use. For details write to Special Sales Manager at the Publisher's address

Library of Congress Cataloging-in-Publication Data
McLaughlin, Paul G.
    Illustrated Ford pickup buyer's guide / Paul G. McLaughlin.
        p.   cm.—(Motorbooks International illustrated buyer's guide series)
    ISBN 0-87938-526-X
    1. Ford trucks—Purchasing.   2. Ford trucks—Collectors and collecting.
    I. Title.   II. Series.
    TL230.5.F57M385 1991
    629.223—dc20   91-9368

On the front cover: A classic Ford pickup and a modern workhorse. The 1956 F-100 with stock farm equipment is owned by Al Whitcombe of Ambler, Pennsylvania. The 1991 F-150 XLT 4 x 4 is courtesy of Haldeman Ford of Kutztown, Pennsylvania. *Mike Mueller*

Printed and bound in the United States of America

Contents

Acknowledgments

In writing this book I had quite a bit of help, and I would like to take this opportunity to thank the following individuals for their assistance:

Bernice McLaughlin, Albuquerque, NM
Ken and Betty Campbell, Albuquerque, NM
Paul G. McLaughlin, Sr., Arlington, MA
Robert Lucero, DDS, Albuquerque, NM
John Emmert, Ford Motor Company, Dearborn, MI
Archie Lewis, Albuquerque, NM
Gayle Warnock, Scottsdale, AZ
Don Bunn, Eden Prairie, MN
Dick Copello, York, PA
Michael MacSems, Olympia, WA
Jerry Bougher, Albany, OR

Eddie Corbin, Albuquerque, NM
Elliott Kahn, Clearwater Beach, FL
Rick Louderbough, Albuquerque, NM
Wayne Smith, Trujillo Creek, CO
Michael Gonzales, Albuquerque, NM
Dan Olsen, Quakertown, PA
George Hinds, Cambridge, MA
Dana Jones, Mills, WY
Charles Jensen, Joliet, IL
Bob Langworthy, Stonington, CT
Harlan Appelquist, Edina, MN
John T. Wierzbicki, Philadelphia, PA
Gary Hallett, Australia

Paul G. McLaughlin
Albuquerque, New Mexico
November 5, 1990

1905-1919 Pioneer Commercials

Although the Ford Motor Company didn't officially start building trucks until the 1917 model year, it was involved in the commercial end of the market before that time, both with products it built and with products that were converted by outside firms.

Ford's first commercial vehicle was released in 1905 and called the Ford delivery car. This model was based on Ford's Model C platform and was no more than a Model C runabout to which a box-type body had been fastened. These delivery cars cost around $950 fob Detroit and weren't a rousing success. Company records dating to this time show that probably fewer than a dozen of them were built.

Ford stayed away from any commercial offerings in 1906 but came back in 1907 with a new delivery van. This one was based on Ford's Model N, and it was a little more successful than its 1905 counterpart. Still customers weren't knocking down the doors to buy these types of vehicles.

Commercial vehicle interest really perked up when the Model T Ford arrived on the automotive scene in 1908. In a short period of time these vehicles gained a reputation for being strong, inexpensive, dependable, and tough enough to go anywhere and do anything asked of them. They were the perfect vehicles to convert for commercial purposes, and convert them people did.

The most popular Model T Ford for conversion purposes was the roadster. All sorts of boxes and pickup beds that were offered by the aftermarket could easily be bolted to the back side of these universal vehicles. Though the roadsters couldn't carry heavy loads, as big trucks did, they could handle thousands of little jobs and were a common sight on city streets during this time. Quite a few were used to deliver goods for hardware stores, bakeries, dairies, department stores and the like.

In 1912 the Ford Motor Company decided to try out the commercial market waters again by offering its customers two factory-

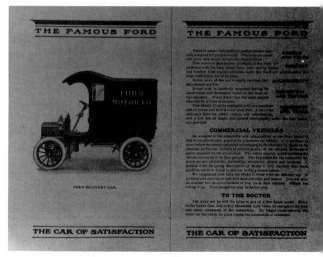

This was one of the earliest Ford advertisements to appear in print, in 1905. Note that the ad even mentions commercial cars. *Michael MacSems collection*

This Model T Ford chemical and hose fire engine has enough equipment on board to fight any fire. Bells, whistles, ladders and hoses were ready to really take control.

cataloged models specifically designed for this segment. One was called the commercial roadster and retailed for about $590; the other was called the Model T delivery car and cost about $700. The commercial roadster, a new offering in 1912, came equipped with a rumble seat that could easily be removed and replaced by a pickup box or bed. The Model T delivery car looked similar to the 1905 delivery car but featured a unique body rather than a bolt-on top. These models had been thoroughly field-tested before their release in 1912 because the Ford Motor Company had supplied some of them to the Bell Telephone System for use as service trucks. Once again customers weren't all that impressed and sales weren't high. Ford was selling every Model T it could build back then, however, so this setback didn't really bother the company.

Though Ford USA was rather skeptical about making a commitment to the commercial market, its Canadian branch felt differently because it was building trucks in its plants for its own, as well as worldwide, markets.

Not content with just supplying bodies to be fitted to Model T chassis, some companies started to offer kits to lengthen and strengthen the Model T frame so it could carry longer and heavier loads. Two major concerns that offered such kits were the A. O. Smith Company and Union Truck Manufacturing. The most famous conversion was the Smith Form-A-Truck kit, which offered an extended steel frame, a heavy-duty-rated two-piece drive shaft, a set of rear leaf springs, solid rubber rear tires and heavy-duty wheels for the rear, and in some cases a heavy-duty chain-driven rear axle. These trucks were popular because they allowed a multitude of extended-length

A 1950s World On Wheels card displaying a 1910 Ford Model T commercial roadster.

bodies to be used on what was otherwise a small, light-duty platform.

Another popular conversion done on Model Ts during this time involved the installation of firefighting bodies and equipment. Manufacturers like the American LaFrance company liked the Model T chassis because of its light weight and its high ground clearance, which allowed it to go into areas that were prohibitive to other heavier automobiles. These vehicles had a much faster response time to fire emergencies than did heavier units or even horse-drawn bodies. Most of these Model T converted rigs were called chemical and hose cars because they usually carried fire extinguishers and a hose reel. Some were plain; others carried a full complement of bells and whistles, and maybe a ladder or two. Some even pulled double duty, serving as the fire chief's car in towns that couldn't afford both a truck and a car. Back in the teens and twenties these chemical and hose cars saw widespread use throughout the United States and parts of Canada too.

Bowing to demand Ford started to offer a bare Model T chassis to customers who wanted to use it for fitting custom-made bodies. Most of the bodies that were put on these bare chassis were the closed variety. They included the delivery van type, ambulances, school buses and the like. These bare chassis models, though still considered automobiles, were the forerunners of Ford's truck models, which would make their debut in 1917.

This newspaper ad for the Ford Model T chassis was a regional ad used in California. *Jerry Bougher*

1917–1919

By 1917 America's trucking industry was growing by leaps and bounds and Henry Ford could no longer ignore this market segment. The potential for sales of commercial vehicles in the United States, as well as the world, was limitless. So beginning in the summer of 1917 the Ford Motor Company officially entered the world of trucking with the release of a new one-ton production chassis. This was in addition to the automobile chassis that had been out for some time.

Nothing too complicated about this 1912 Model T delivery car. It has a straightforward approach with a semi-open body painted in a nice shade of dark blue, highlighted by shiny brass and wide white tires. *Dan Olsen*

A mostly original, 6,600 mile 1915 Model T pie wagon. *Bob Langworthy*

A 1915 Model T delivery car operated by Tasty-kake. *Dan Olsen*

By taking this step Henry Ford was able to attract buyers who needed a lightweight vehicle as well as the buyer who needed something a little more substantial than a car chassis.

Ford's one-ton chassis was similar in concept to the conversion units in that it was longer and stronger than a passenger-car-type frame. The wheelbase was longer by 24 in., and on the back side of these trucks you could find a worm-drive rear axle suspended on a set of longitudinal leaf springs. Rear tires were of solid rubber and wheels, like those on the conversions, were of the artillery type. The availability of such a chassis from the Ford factory probably sounded the death knell for converters with products like the Smith Form-A-Truck. Why go to all the bother of having a car chassis converted when all you had to do was order one from your local Ford agent, and probably at a lower cost?

In late 1917 America entered the First World War and Henry Ford, a disillusioned pacifist, put his company and his full support behind the war effort. This effort involved supplying thousands of cars, trucks and ambulances, and even some boats, to help defeat the Axis powers in Europe. One well-known vehicle to come out of this conflict was the Model T Ford ambulance. Examples of this workhorse were seen on battlefields all over Europe, running here, there and everywhere transporting thousands of wounded soldiers from the battlefronts to army hospitals. They more than earned their keep and became legends for what they could do under the worst possible conditions then known to humankind. These ambulances were built to US Army specifications on Model T car chassis, and Ford built more than 5,700 of them before the hostilities were over.

Though a war was going on worldwide, civilian vehicle production still continued—a situation unlike what would happen during

This racy Model T roadster pickup has been
outfitted with cream-colored wire wheels and a
Gilmore Red Lion gasoline tire cover.

World War II when America's automobile
factories were turned over completely to
war material production. A business boom
was going on in the United States and
demand for automobiles and trucks was at a
fever pitch. Henry Ford's factory was putting out more Model T vehicles than it had
before, and a lot of them were being fitted
with commercial-type bodies. Ford's new
Model TT (Tonner Truck) with a runabout
factory cab or just the bare chassis alone was
finding favor with all sorts of body companies and businesses. These new vehicles
were so popular that before the decade was
out Ford had sold more than 100,000 commercial chassis.

In the teens two items of interest would
have a profound effect on the future of the
company. In 1919 the Ford Motor Company
under the auspices of Henry Ford bought
out all its minority stockholders, thus be-
coming 100-percent family owned. Henry
Ford did this so he wouldn't have to deal
with anybody else on how to run the company or what sort of products to build. He
was fiercely independent and he wanted his
company to be so too.

The other item of note occurring in 1919
involved the start of the development of a
land parcel that would one day grow into the
largest industrial manufacturing complex of
its kind in the world. This parcel of land ran

A 1918 Model T delivery car that once plied its trade on the streets of Jamaica, New York. The body is green, while the hood, fenders, running boards and radiator are black. Whitewall tires add a nice touch. *Dan Olsen*

Model T gasoline trucks like this restored 1915 model once roamed American roads in great numbers. Now they are a rare breed, especially ones that look as nice as this particular example.

alongside the River Rouge and would be called upon its completion the Rouge Plant. The day the first shovelful of dirt was turned over, Henry Ford looked out over the land and envisioned a place where raw materials would go in one end and completed automobiles would come out the other end.

When completed, the Rouge Plant was like a large self-sufficient city, a place that provided work for thousands of Ford employees down through the years. A place that also produced some of the most memorable cars and trucks that ever turned a wheel on the highways and byways of the world.

A Model T delivery car from the backside.
Archie Lewis

Chapter 2

1920–1927
Model T
Commercials

| ★★★ | 1920–1927 Model T with aftermarket commercial body |
| ★★★★ | 1925–1927 Model T Runabout with pickup body |

The new decade of the twenties started out on a negative note for the Ford Motor Company. In retrospect it would prove to be like a roller coaster ride for Ford, full of highs and lows.

A recession greeted American businesses in 1921, and Henry Ford surely felt the pinch. Auto sales were down, and money around his company was hard to find, since Ford had spent quite a bit of cash to buy out his minority stockholders in 1919. Facing the situation squarely Ford cut prices, cut back on production and idled some of his workers. But nothing seemed to bring the auto business out of its doldrums. Feeling desperate Ford even went to see his old nemeses, the bankers, to see if he could arrange some loans. Knowing full well that Ford didn't hold them in high esteem the bankers declined to help and instead took relish in the idea that Ford had finally gotten enough rope to hang himself. However, Ford wasn't finished pulling rabbits out of his hat and performing other tricks to keep his company afloat.

The auto magnate's saviors this time around were his agents and dealers scattered throughout the United States. Ford dumped his problem in their lap. He sold them vehicles they didn't order, and it was up to them to find buyers. Needless to say, they were in hotter water than he was, but they accepted this move grudgingly in order not to lose their franchises. Ford got rid of his cars, got some money to pay his bills, and came out smelling like a rose when all was said and done.

Ford's money problems were the least of his troubles as the twenties progressed. Two events in 1921 would have a profound effect on the fortunes of the Ford Motor Company before the decade was over. The first event revolved around the Dodge brothers, who at one time were suppliers to Ford as well as

If you were a telephone lineman in 1921 you might have driven a Model T Bell Telephone System truck like this one.

being major stockholders in his company. Ford didn't particularly care for John and Horace Dodge, and the same could be said of them. Ford and the Dodge brothers always seemed to be involved in some sort of confrontation. Ford wanted the Dodges out of his company, and when the opportunity presented itself he bought them out lock, stock and barrel. The Dodge brothers made quite a tidy sum on this exchange and invested it in a company of their own to compete against Ford. In 1921 they also became the sole distributor of Graham Brothers trucks. Eventually the Dodges would buy out the Grahams and start to build a company that would go toe to toe with Ford for light-duty truck sales.

That was a serious situation, but it paled in comparison with an event that befell Ford when one of his right-hand men, William Knudsen, left after a dispute. Knudsen was an important player in the world of Ford

Motor Company because he was Ford's production boss. Knudsen knew the automobile business inside and out, and his departure caused Ford some consternation. As if that wasn't bad enough, Knudsen went across town and took the head position at Chevrolet, much as Lee Iacocca did in the seventies.

Chevrolet, like Chrysler later, was in dire straits in the early twenties, and the bosses at General Motors were seriously considering disbanding the company and redistributing its assets to their other companies. But Knudsen came in and started cutting here, there and everywhere, and pretty soon the battered and bruised company was showing signs of renewed life. This turnaround was nothing short of miraculous, and pretty soon Chevrolet was competing with Ford Motor Company again, this time in a stronger position.

Within six years Chevrolet had gone from

a down-and-out company to a healthy and robust entity that could match Ford sale for sale. And when the Model T assembly plants were shut down for conversion to Model A production Chevrolet surpassed Ford for sales supremacy. Chevrolet got by and never looked back and held Ford at bay for almost sixty years. It was only in the last few model years of the eighties that the tables turned and Ford sat in the top position.

If 1921 was a low point for Ford, 1922 was a banner year for the production of Ford cars and trucks. Truck chassis production topped 127,300 units. Ford sold so many of them because they were priced so low. You could buy a stripped Model T car chassis for about $230, whereas a stripped TT chassis was priced at $420. These prices were quite a savings over the cost charged for similar items the year before. A buyer received a fully equipped chassis with drivetrain, front fenders, hood, cowl, dashboard, running boards, magneto headlamps, horn, tools and an oil-fired taillight. Quite a bargain when

A sharp Model TT wrecker, shown at a 1986 truck show. This one has a blue-painted radiator, hood, fenders and boom. A clear-coat finish was applied to the cab and body to show off the natural beauty of the wood. *Dan Olsen*

This colorful Model T C cab truck sits outside of an Indian trading post in southeastern New Mexico.

you consider what the competition was offering.

Aftermarket bodies for these truck chas-

A vintage Model T closed-cab wrecker dating from the 1920s. It is equipped with heavier wheels on its backside. *Don Bunn*

sis were available from major suppliers like Columbia Motor Company, Martin-Parry, Mifflinburg Body Company, Calumet, Galion, Atlas Motor Truck Company, Boyertown Auto Body Works and the like. Prices for bodies ran anywhere from $50 for the simplest to more than $500 for the more involved. In addition to these offerings other bodies were sold by smaller outfits, and some bodies were even custom crafted by cabinetmakers and blacksmiths. The truck body business was a pretty lucrative affair back in the twenties.

To make truck operations a little simpler electric starting and demountable rims came on line about this time, and Ford offered them as options. It was easy to spot an electric-starter-equipped truck from the outside because it carried its batteries in a box by its running boards for easy access. These batteries were used just to start the trucks or cars; headlights and taillights were

This Model T closed-cab truck features a unique right-window treatment with a small glass oval in a wooden panel.

still being powered by magnetos running off the engines.

Things got better for Ford in 1923, as TT chassis production grew to more than 193,200 units. Truck production in Canada was up also, as more than 32,000 trucks were built and sold north of the US-Canada border. The major issue helping to fuel these gains probably was the lower prices Ford was asking for its Model T cars and truck chassis.

The big news at Ford Motor Company in 1924 was the announcement that Ford was going to start offering its own cataloged bodies as an addition to its stripped Model T and TT chassis. Before this announcement, putting bodies on Ford commercial vehicles was the exclusive domain of aftermarket suppliers. It was said that Henry Ford held out from getting involved in this aspect of the business because he feared a backlash from his customers. Evidently that fear had subsided when 1924 rolled around.

Ford's first body was an express pickup type made of steel. It was shipped to Ford dealers in a knocked-down version for them to assemble later. These bodies were painted black to match the color used on the cabs and fenders if so equipped. By the end of the model year Ford was offering eight bodies, most of them being derivatives of the express pickup body.

Another new item from Ford in 1924 was the introduction of the semiclosed C-cab in addition to the normal runabout cab that was offered and bought by most buyers who wanted a Ford-sourced cab. The Model T also featured a redesign in the radiator and hood areas. Specifically, the radiator was a bit taller, as was the hood, which now blended in with the cowl better.

For 1925 Henry Ford outdid himself as far as his trucking customers were concerned. His first feat came at the beginning of the model year when he announced a new 8 ft. stake-and-platform body would be available for the Model T. The body was also offered as just a platform for those who didn't need the stakes.

Surprise number two arrived with the release of a fully enclosed cab for TT models, in addition to the C-type cab. The difference in price between the two amounted to $20. For that sum the closed cab buyer received a fully enclosed steel cab with two doors with plate glass windows, an adjustable windshield, a dispatch box and a rubber floor mat. The real bonus this cab offered, though, was better protection from the elements, especially in the winter.

Next on the agenda was a notice that on April 25, 1925, a new factory commercial vehicle would be introduced. This vehicle would be the first of millions to follow, for it was Ford's first pickup truck offering. Officially it was called the Ford Model T runabout with pickup body. And it was available

fob Detroit for $281. For that price a buyer received a sporty-looking pickup roadster with an all-steel pickup bed box. The box wasn't as long as the express box used on the Model TT, but it nevertheless got its job done by providing the businessman or farmer with a way to get goods or services to market. These new models were so popular that before the model year was out Ford had sold almost 33,800 of them.

Ford also made some changes this year that helped ease the burden of driving and maintaining these vehicles. Modifications like an improved oiling system, a quicker, 5:1 steering ratio and a few other items made life a lot easier for the trucker.

All told, these changes helped Ford to have its best model year yet. Ford truck sales were growing steadily, and by 1926 it was estimated that the Ford Motor Company had a

A Model T truck equipped with a platform/stake body. Note the sliding cab door. *Dan Olsen*

Before Ford released their factory-built station wagons in 1929, a buyer had to purchase a cowl and chassis model and then have an aftermarket Depot Hack body installed, like this one. This is a 1926 model. *Dan Olsen*

phenomenal seventy-five percent of the truck market.

Even though his production records didn't show it, Henry Ford was starting to read the writing on the wall. For years his Ford vehicles were so far ahead of the rest he had plenty of breathing room. But the winds of change were blowing from a different direction in the late twenties, and what had made the Model T Fords so appealing before now helped to usher in their downfall. People didn't want simple, dependable, cheap vehicles anymore. They wanted vehicles that came with a little pizzazz, and more convenience features. For a few dollars more, Ford's competitors seemed to be offering better vehicles, and because of that percep-

tion his customers and noncustomers alike were starting to buy elsewhere, and that was helping to narrow the gap between his company and the others. So in 1925 Ford gave the word to start developing a new model, and until that new model was ready to release he would continue to sell his beloved Model T.

Ford knew that he couldn't sell his Model Ts now without a gimmick, and that gimmick in 1926 involved advertising the new Model T as a vehicle that featured more than eighty changes. It's hard to say if the Model T really had eighty changes or not, but the most dramatic changes were readily apparent on the body. It had a new fender design, a longer and taller hood, a revision of the cowl,

A Model T camper from the 1920s. *Charles Jensen collection*

A 1926 Fordson stake model. Ford produced few of these trucks; the production total is believed to be in the single-digit range.

A Shriner group aboard their Model T fire engine.

wider running boards, more hood louver vents and an air vent on top of the cowl. Ford started to mount the headlights and taillights on the fenders rather than on the frame rails, as was previously done. A new, nickel-plated radiator grille was offered as standard equipment on the closed cars and as optional equipment on all the rest. Other changes involved a switch over to a larger steering wheel, redesigned foot pedals and larger parking brakes. Ford also reworked the chassis and suspension systems that lowered the new Model T Ford by 1½ in. And in a reversal of his "any color as long as it is black" policy, some Model Ts were now offered in colors like gray, brown and blue.

Ford and his company spent a lot of time, money and effort to spruce up the Model T. That dressing up helped to sell a few more Model Ts, including the Model T with pickup body. In 1926 these popular trucks themselves accounted for more than 75,400 Model T sales. Total truck sales this year for Ford amounted to about 186,000 units, which wasn't a bad performance for such an outdated model.

For 1927, the last year of the Model T, changes were kept to a minimum, and these models were virtually the same as their 1926 counterparts. One modification concerned the electric starter, which was now a standard piece of equipment clear across the board.

In May of 1927, just after the 15 millionth Model T was produced, Henry Ford gave the word to start cutting back, and in June the plug was officially pulled on Model T production. The plants were closed for almost six months while the conversion was going on to build the Model A and Model AA Fords, worthy successors to the Model T that had served Ford—and his customers too—so well for almost nineteen years.

Chapter 3

1928–1931 Model A Commercials

The Model A Fords that were released in December 1927 as 1928 models were a much-needed shot in the arm for Ford. Though the Model T was a worthy vehicle, it no longer held mass appeal, for buyers wanted cars and trucks that were stylish and easier to operate. People wanted more choices in colors, they wanted electric starting, and they wanted cars and trucks with transmissions that shifted like those in other cars. They also wanted more power and

A 1928 Model A roadster pickup in Kauai, Hawaii.

more prestige than the Model T could offer, and they got all that and more with the Model A.

These new vehicles were so smart looking that some people thought of them as Baby Lincolns because some of their stylish lines mimicked the Lincoln's. A good share of the credit for producing such a fine-looking Ford went to Edsel Ford, Henry Ford's only son. Henry Ford was good with the mechanical side of the house, but when it came to styling Edsel Ford was head and shoulders over his dad.

During the Model A years Ford trucks were separated into two classes. The light-duty range of trucks and related vehicles was called the Ford commercial car line, and the one-ton rated trucks were called the Model AA vehicles. Both series of trucks used the same running gear, hood, fenders, cowl, radiators and the like. The only differences between the two involved wheelbase length, frame length, springs, wheels, shocks and axles.

Whatever the size or series, both types of vehicles were available, in most cases, in either an open- or a closed-cab form. For the first few months of production, though, finding a closed-cab version was rather difficult. When it did become available in large enough numbers the closed-cab version was by far the cab of choice because the difference in price between the two was low.

A popular feature found on this new Ford was its powerplant, a newly designed

A 1930 Model A station wagon restored with popular era accessories like whitewall tires and a Quail radiator mascot. *Elliott Kahn*

200.5 ci four-cylinder engine that put out 40 hp—enough power, especially in the car and light-duty truck line, to give spritely performance. This engine included a thermo-syphon cooling system, a splash-type lubrication system with an oil pump, a forged-steel crankshaft, aluminum pistons and a battery-powered ignition system. Fuel was supplied to a Zenith one-barrel updraft carburetor from a cowl-mounted 10 gallon fuel tank.

Making a quantum leap from the Model T's planetary transmission the new Model A and Model AAs featured a new H-patterned three-speed manual transmission. Shifting chores were accomplished by means of a floor-mounted lever and a double-disc clutch setup that was replaced by a single-disc unit

later in the model year. The torque-tube rear ends looked the same as the Model T units, but the units used in Model A and Model AA vehicles were beefed up substantially.

Most of the Ford commercial vehicles produced during the late twenties and early thirties featured black-painted radiator shells, headlamp buckets and running boards. The Model A cars featured nickel-plated radiator shells as standard equipment and other brightwork too. Some of those items found their way onto some Ford pickups during this time and since, because their owners wanted to brighten up their looks. Most Ford commercial vehicles of this period also featured green cabs and bodies as standard Ford fare.

A 1930 Model A roadster pickup finished, as most commercial vehicles were back then, in green with black fenders, radiator and top.

The best of both worlds. Two Model A pickups; one is restored while the other has been customized.

Model A deluxe delivery cars.

The commercial car line-up in 1928 consisted of open- and closed-cab pickups, panel deliveries and chassis models.

The same line-up appeared for 1929 except that two more light-duty commercial vehicles were added. These new models were called the station wagon and the taxi-cab. The former was the world's first mass-produced station wagon from a manufacturer; the latter was a four-door model that featured a partition that separated the driver from the passenger compartment.

Before the introduction of Ford's station wagon, if one wanted such a vehicle one had to purchase a Depot Hack body from an aftermarket source and have it mounted on a bare chassis. Now all one had to do was place an order with a Ford dealer. These commercial cars featured bodies made from hard maple with birch paneling. The bodies were built by Murray Body and Fender Company from raw materials supplied by Ford's Iron Mountain forests located on the Upper Peninsula of Michigan. These vehicles also featured Manila Brown paint on their cowl and hood, and black-painted run-

ning boards. Cost for this model in 1929 was about $695.

Ford was also in the taxicab business throughout 1929 and into 1930. In all it pro-

Model A truck with express-type pickup box and a C cab body.

An unrestored 1929 Model A with a special bus body.

duced about 5,300 taxis during this period before it dropped this model from its catalogs. The taxicab model could carry three passengers on the back seat; a fourth passenger could be accommodated if necessary by a fold-down jump seat that was stored out of the way when not in use. Luggage was carried in the area usually provided for a front-seat passenger or in a rack mounted on the roof. These models also came equipped with Taximeter equipment as part of their standard fare.

Another closed commercial vehicle offering in 1929 was the Deluxe delivery car, which was based on a two-door sedan body configuration. This model was trimmed out like a regular sedan and was available in sedan colors rather than just commercial choices. It had one large rear door for loading, and its rear sedan window openings were covered by steel panels. Inside its walls were covered by Masonite panels and its seats were covered in a brown-toned artificial leather just like that used in panel delivery models.

1929–1930 Prices

Model	Price
Model A Deluxe delivery car	$595
Model A closed or open cab pickup	$445
Model A panel delivery	$575
Station wagon	$695
Taxicab	$800
Model A commercial chassis	$350
Model A platform	NA
Model A stake	NA

For 1930 the Model As underwent a re-styling job that was most noticeable on the front end. The new Model As featured a wider, redesigned cowl that now covered the lower A-pillars. A taller, thinner radiator shell also graced the new front end, a shell that was now stamped out of stainless steel rather than being nickel plated. With the taller radiator came a taller hood with a higher hoodline that helped integrate the whole front end into a more cohesive unit. Headlamps and fenders were updated too, also helping to give the new Model A design a more modern look.

Since they were based on car models, Ford's light-duty trucks also received these trim updates. The larger trucks still used the earlier trim pieces until the supplies were exhausted.

For 1931 the Model A Fords received some minor design changes, and a couple of new models graced this year's commercial car catalogs. One of these new models was called the Model A Deluxe pickup. This unique model featured a special body supplied to Ford by the Briggs Manufacturing Company. Most of these units were painted white with black fenders and running boards. What set these vehicles apart from the regular version was a special high, slab-

A Model A truck with a US Mail body that once saw service on the streets of Enid, Oklahoma.

This 1931 Model A roadster with stake body is a
rare sight today.

This Model A roadster pickup competed in the
1990 Great American Cross Country Race.

This Model A closed-cab pickup needs a little tender loving care to make it look as nice as it did back in the late 1920s.

sided body that came with a special tailgate and a wood-lined cargo area. This body was bolted to the back side of a closed-cab body so it looked like an integral cab and body model that Ford used in the sixties. These special pickups featured nickel-plated radiator shells and headlamp buckets. They also used carlike cowl lamps and chrome-plated grab rails that were mounted atop the pickup bed box sides.

Another unique new model that was offered this year was the town car delivery, which was meant to appeal to businesses that wanted a chic delivery vehicle. This version of the Model A commercial car line looked as if it was designed for the carriage trade. It featured a custom aluminum body

A beautifully restored Model A roadster pickup.
Elliott Kahn

A Model A dump truck.

with a rakish sloping windshield, cowl lamps, nickel-plated trim, dual side-mounted spare tires and a sliding door into the cargo area from behind the seats. The driver's compartment was open like that in a chauffeured limousine and featured black-leather-covered seats. In addition the cargo area was carpeted, as any vehicle of this nature should be. Ford originally produced some 200 of these vehicles in 1930, and they are rather hard to come by today. Ford also offered these vehicles in 1931, but dropped them after that.

For cleaning establishments and other businesses that needed a little extra height in their delivery vehicles Ford had just the ticket in 1931 with a new drop-floor panel model. As its name suggested, this panel truck featured a lower floor than that on the regular panel truck.

Another special model was called the Model A special delivery, or the natural wood panel delivery. Baker-Raulang Company supplied Ford with this body, which had a design similar to the station wagon's. Like the station wagon, the special delivery featured a maple and birch paneled body, but unlike the station wagon it was a two-door rather than a four-door.

In addition to these specialty models Ford offered the commercial buyer a complete line of regular commercial vehicles ranging from a bare chassis to stake-bodied workhorses.

The Model A and Model AA vehicles served Ford well during the short time they were in production. They helped bridge the gap between the obsolete Model Ts and the ever-changing Ford trucks that followed.

A 1931 Model A closed-cab "Huckster" pickup—
a rare sight today on the street or at car shows.

A Model A fire truck.

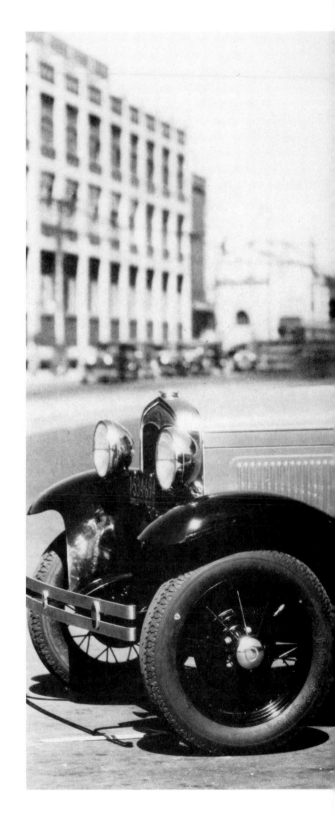

A classy 1931 Model A Deluxe delivery car that once belonged to the Pillsbury Flour Mills. *Ford Motor Company*

Chapter 4

1932-1939 V-8 Commercials

★★★★★	1932-1939 Station wagon
★★★	1932-1939 Sedan delivery
★★	1932-1939 Panel delivery
★★★★★	1932-1934 Open-cab pickup
★★★★★	1932-1939 Closed-cab pickup
★★★	1936-1939 Marmon-Herrington all-wheel-drive
★★★	1939 Platform/stake

We Americans didn't have too much to cheer about in 1932, the worst year of the Depression. A large number of people were still out of work, money was scarce for most and more people were showing up in bread lines every day. It was a bleak time, but hopeful signs were on the horizon and we were about to turn a corner and head out in the direction of prosperity. Frankin Roosevelt had just been elected president, and in 1933 he would start to lead us away from the land of doom and gloom out toward the valley of hope.

In the midst of such hard times the last thing most people had on their mind was to purchase a new car or truck. After all, they had more important concerns to worry about in the early thirties than cars. The car makers were well aware of this climate because their ledgers showed that sales were way down, as were their profit margins.

It wasn't the best time to launch a new automobile, but Henry Ford figured the automotive world needed a jolt, and in March of 1932 the thunderbolt struck in the form of the newly designed Model 18 Ford. The 1 in that designation stood for "the first," and the 8 stood for the number of cylinders in the engine. So the 1932 Ford was the first such Ford to carry an eight-cylinder engine.

Old Henry shocked the world with his release of the now famous Ford flathead V-8, but the V-8 engines weren't a new idea by any means. As a matter of fact Ford's

chief rival Chevrolet had a V-8 option for a short time in the teens. But this Chevrolet engine was cumbersome to build and not economical to operate, and a car so equipped was expensive to boot. Needless to say it didn't prove too popular. Ford's new V-8, on the other hand, was simple to produce and pretty straightforward in its approach to propelling an automobile. It was powerful and relatively economical to operate when compared with other eight-cylinder engines

---

1932 Ford Four-Cylinder Engine
Type: 4 cylinder L-design
Cylinders: 4 cast in block
Bore x stroke: 3⅞ in. x 4¼ in.
Weight: 454 lb
Firing order: 1, 2, 3, 4
Brake horsepower: 50 bhp at 2800 rpm
Torque: 128 lb-ft at 1400 rpm
Displacement: 200.5 ci
Compression ratio: 4.6:1
Main bearings: 3
Pistons: Aluminum
Crankcase capacity: 5 quarts
Spark plugs: ⅞ in. straight thread
Generator: 2 pole
Carburetor: Ford Zenith
Starter: Bendix drive
Fan: 2 blade
Water pump: 3 blade
Clutch: Dry disc, single plate

A restored 1932 Ford Model B station wagon.
Elliott Kahn

of this period. The best part of the engine was that it was in a low-price Ford. So it was affordable for anybody who had the means to buy a car in 1932.

Going from a four-cylinder powerplant to a V-8 was a quantum leap in automotive circles back in the thirties. And some people probably thought that Henry Ford might have overstepped the boundaries of good sense, considering the gloomy automotive climate of the period. But Ford was crafty as a fox, and his turning to the V-8 allowed him to stay one step ahead of his arch rivals over at Chevrolet. Chevrolet had beaten the four-cylinder Ford by offering a six-cylinder engine for a few dollars more. Now the tables in the power game were turned, with the edge going decidedly in Ford's direction—an edge his company would enjoy for almost a quarter of a century.

Ford was well aware that he couldn't win this game on sheer mechanicals alone, so he wrapped that V-8 in a new rendition of the

Baby Lincoln Model A Ford styling. These new Fords were so well received from a styling standpoint that they were still revered by automotive enthusiasts almost sixty years later.

Ford was also smart enough to know that not everyone wanted a V-8, especially one so new. So for those folks he also made available a four-cylinder-powered version. This was called the Model B Ford, and it was powered by an upgraded Model A engine that now put out an extra 10 hp. The Model B powerplant displaced 200.5 ci and put out 50 hp in 1932, whereas the new V-8 displaced 221 ci and was rated at 65 hp at 3400 rpm. The difference in price between the two amounted to only about $10, and the V-8 car outsold the four-cylinder version by a margin of two to one.

At first Ford envisioned his V-8 to be just a powerplant for his cars, whereas the tried-and-true four-cylinder engine would continue to be his mainstay in the commercial

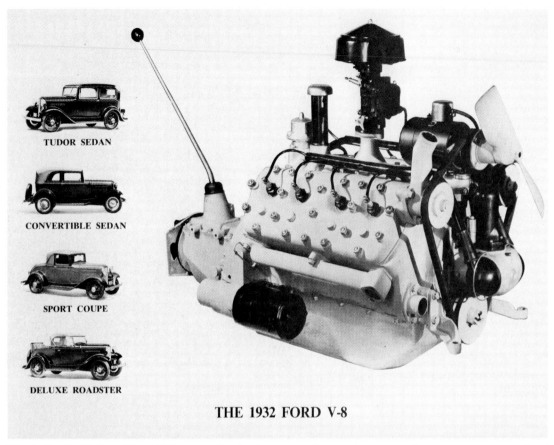

TUDOR SEDAN

CONVERTIBLE SEDAN

SPORT COUPE

DELUXE ROADSTER

THE 1932 FORD V-8

The fantastic Flathead Ford V-8, an engine that served the Ford Motor Company well in car and truck use for more than twenty years. *Ford Motor Company*

field. His V-8 proved so popular that his truck customers wanted in on the action too. They implored the manufacturer to release the engine for commercial use also. The only problem Ford faced at that moment was that demand for the V-8 far exceeded supply, so he couldn't defer to their wishes right away. But toward the end of the model year some V-8s found their way into his trucks. For the most part, however, four-cylinder Model B engines in 1932 Ford commercial vehicles are the norm rather than the exception. And the 1932 commercial owner who does have an original V-8 engined vehicle has something to be treasured.

The commercial car line in 1932 consisted of redesigned pickups in open and closed forms, station wagons, panel deliveries, cab-and-chassis models, and bare chassis.

In retrospect, though 1932 overall was a bad year for the automotive marketplace in general, automotive history has treated Henry Ford very well because of his much beloved Deuce.

1933–1934
By the time the 1933 model year was in top gear the supply of Ford V-8 engines had grown considerably, so Henry Ford's limits were lifted and anyone who wanted one could now have a V-8 under a Ford hood. Whether that hood was on a car or a truck didn't matter anymore.

A 1933 Ford closed-cab V-8 truck with a home-made platform body.

Ford felt that owing to its more economical nature the four-cylinder engine would be the engine of choice for commercial users, especially people who had vehicles in the light-duty range. But Ford's instincts missed the mark by a wide margin, as most people opted for the V-8. And who could blame them with the V-8 costing only about $50 more than a similarly equipped four-cylinder truck?

1934 Production

Model	4 cylinder	V-8
Sedan delivery	483	9,328
Station wagon	95	2,905
Open-cab pickup	248	99
Closed-cab pickup	13,914	66,922
Chassis	NA	NA
Chassis with cab	NA	NA

Ford Motor Company spent quite a large sum of money to redesign its 1933 car line, and the end result of its efforts was quite pleasing to the eye. The 1933 Fords, and the similar-looking 1934 models, were some of the sharpest-looking Fords ever produced. It's a shame Ford didn't sell more of them back then so we would have more of them around today to enjoy.

Since the sedan delivery and station wagon models were based on car designs, they received the new front-end treatment of the regular car line, whereas the pickups, panels and the like retained the styling cues of their 1932 counterparts. Though similar in appearance, the two lines were differentiated by some changes. One change involved an increase in the wheelbase from 106 to 112 in., which helped to shorten the rear overhang, giving these trucks a more balanced appearance. Another change involved tilting the top of the radiator grille shell back about 5 degrees. For pickup truck buyers the floor in the bed was now made of steel with a wooden underlay panel. Before this modification pickup bed floors were made of wood slats that were separated by steel skid strips.

Prices for Ford's commercial car line in 1933 ranged from a low of $320 for a four-cylinder Model C chassis to a high of $670 for a Deluxe station wagon. The panel delivery, when powered by a four-cylinder engine, could be had for $510, and the pickup with a four was available for $440. The pickups could be had in open or closed form, with the closed-cab version being a lot more popular than its open, roadster-style counterpart.

For the panel delivery buyer two choices were available, the Standard model for $510 and the Deluxe at $530. Both models offered the buyer a highly styled, closed delivery vehicle. The cargo area featured a hardwood floor with steel rub strips to make loading much easier. Steel panels on the lower inside body panels helped to protect these panels from damage caused by load shifts. Hardwood vertical posts and horizontal slats were used in the roof area for added protection and to give a little more structural integrity to the body. On the back side a welded steel frame held a set of double steel loading doors.

For the additional $20 the Deluxe buyer got Masonite side panels in the cargo area and an artificial-leather-covered headliner that gave this version a more finished appearance. On the outside the Deluxe models carried side panel moldings, chrome-plated cowl lamps, a chrome-plated front bumper, a rear side mirror and a chrome-plated wiper. They also had a highly polished paint finish that was a lot brighter than the paint used on the Standard version.

The sedan delivery, being a Ford automobile derivative, looked more like a passenger car than a commercial car. It had a large,

This 1933 V-8 pickup is one of 33,748 that Ford built that year. Note that this truck carries two front license tags—a modern one and a vintage 1933–1934 tag.

wide cargo door on its back side and an artificial-leather-covered interior in a rich dark brown color. Production numbers show that a grand total of 4,449 of these sedan deliveries were sold in 1933. Production breakdowns show that fifty-two percent of them were V-8 powered, with forty-eight percent having the Model C four-cylinder engine. The V-8 units cost $50 more than the Model C version.

Both engines were updated in 1933, with the four-cylinder engine now being designated the Model C. The V-8 engine, which was prone to overheating, received a set of aluminum heads to help increase its cooling capacity. Both engines were backed up by three-speed manual transmissions.

All the 1934 offerings looked similar to their 1933 counterparts except for some minor trim variations. Though they looked alike on the outside, Ford made a lot of changes to the V-8 engine to make them more economical and more efficient to run. These changes included a different head design that incorporated water-line thermostats, a counterbalanced cast-alloy crankshaft, open-skirt steel pistons, an improved fuel pump and switching of the carburetor from a single-venturi design to a double-venturi design. This two-barrel carburetor alone probably added the 15 extra horsepower found on these engines, which were now rated at 90 hp.

Production of four-cylinder-powered commercial vehicles was even lower in 1934 than in 1933, and this would be the last year for quite a while that Ford would offer such an engine. If someone were looking to buy a low-production 1934 model he or she might want to search out one of these four-cylinder vehicles because, as the 1934 production chart shows, their numbers were far below those of the V-8s.

The only time a four-cylinder-powered vehicle had a larger production number than a V-8 was in an open cab pickup form. The year 1934 was the last for these open cab vehicles too, because Ford felt their low popularity precluded carrying them in its catalogs anymore.

In 1935 Ford built 47,600 pickups like the one pictured here. It has a blue body with black fenders and red wheels.

1935-1936

For Ford 1935 and 1936 were good years for truck sales. In 1935 Ford was the number 1 seller in the United States for both cars and trucks, a feat the company wouldn't accomplish again for many years.

Ford's commercial car line-up featured all-new designs on the car-based, as well as the truck-based, offerings. They sported new grilles, more rounded fenders, more rounded lines on the truck cabs and bodies, longer hoods and new trim pieces.

The trucks were also changed under the skin, especially in the chassis area where the engine was placed in a more forward position. By moving the engine forward Ford could move the cab and bodies forward too, cutting down on the rear-end overhang even more. This modification helped the trucks to better handle their payloads and gave them a better ride whether they were loaded or not.

The 1935 commercial car line consisted of the sedan delivery, deluxe panel delivery, panel delivery, pickup, station wagon, chassis, and chassis-and-cab models.

The sedan delivery accounted for 8,300 sales by itself, a figure that was high for such a specialized model. Its popularity might have had something to do with its handsome new body, which was supplied to Ford by the

A beautiful 1936 Ford sedan delivery gets ready to run another leg of the Great American Cross Country Race in 1987.

Briggs Company. This model featured a load area that was almost 6 ft. in length. Its body was of a three-door design, with the third door being a large, side-opening cargo door.

The station wagon body was another handsome design supplied to Ford by the Murray Company. Murray built these bodies to Ford specifications with wood supplied by Ford's Iron Mountain wood-processing plant, which provided raw materials for all of Ford's wood projects. The station wagon could seat seven passengers on its three seats. A new feature was roll-up glass windows in the front doors; the rest of the window areas were still covered by side curtains of isinglass and canvas construction. The station wagon was still not the most popular entry in this line-up because of the constant wood upkeep that was needed to maintain its beauty.

The panel delivery was available again in a half-ton or one-ton form. The lighter one fell into Ford's commercial car line, whereas

1935–1936 Production

Model	Total
1935	
Pickup	47,639
Sedan delivery	8,308
Station wagon	4,536
Panel	NA
1936	
Station wagon	7,044
Pickup	67,163
Deluxe pickup	2,570
Sedan delivery	7,592
Deluxe sedan delivery	209

1935 Prices

Model	Price
Station wagon	$670
Deluxe ½ ton panel	$580
Standard ½ ton panel	$565
Pickup	$480

1935–1936 Options

Passenger seat (panel and sedan delivery)
Whitewall tires
Roll-down rear window (panel and sedan delivery)
Heater
Radio
Spare tire
Rear bumper
Spare tire cover
Chrome-plated outside rearview mirror
Dual windshield wipers (non-Deluxe models)
Cigar lighter
2 taillights (sedan delivery)
Bumper guards
Special paint treatment
Deluxe trim updates

the larger one was an honest-to-goodness truck. This model was also available as either a Standard version or a Deluxe version. In Standard form it came with a seat for the driver, with a passenger seat as an extra-cost option. Its cargo area floor consisted of a series of hardwood planks separated by some steel skid strips. Longer front and rear springs gave it a better ride than similar vehicles produced before. Once again the inner side of the cargo area was protected from load shift by some hardwood vertical posts and lower-body steel paneling.

In addition to the items found on the Standard model a Deluxe buyer got an aluminum painted grille, color-keyed wheels, a lined interior, twin chrome-plated horns, windshield wipers and chrome-plated rearview mirrors. All this extra equipment came for a low $15 extra.

A restored 1936 Ford school bus.

This 1936 Ford panel delivery van has been restored and is still in daily use as a rolling bill-
board for this small business in the Midwest.

1936 V-8 Engines

V8-60
Displacement: 136 ci
Bore: 2⅗ in.
Stroke: 3⅕ in.
Compression ratio: 6.6:1
Carburetor: 2V downdraft
Horsepower: 60 hp at 3600 rpm

V8-85
Displacement: 221 ci
Bore: 3 1/16 in.
Stroke: 3¾ in.
Compression ratio: 6.3:1
Carburetor: 2V downdraft
Horsepower: 85 hp at 3800 rpm

The pickup model featured a redesigned all-steel cab with a side-mounted spare tire that was moved from the right front fender to a spot directly behind the right door. A steel panel was installed between the pickup box bed and the running board to give the truck sides a more finished appearance. On the front end a new chrome-plated bumper with red pinstripes was added, giving off a much brighter appearance. The pickup, especially when fitted with wide whitewall tires, was now a rakish-looking vehicle.

The only engine available this year for Ford vehicles was the 221 ci V-8 now rated at 85 hp.

For the 1936 model year the Ford Motor Company made some changes to its light-duty commercials to make them even better.

No changes were made in the models offered but some occurred in the equipment they carried. The biggest alteration involved the addition of a smaller V-8 engine to the line-up for those looking for added economy. The larger V-8 was now referred to as the V8-85, and the smaller engine, which featured a smaller bore and stroke, was called the V8-60. This new engine displaced 136 ci and put out 60 hp at 3600 rpm. It was quite a bit more economical than its larger sibling when used in automobiles and light-duty commercials. For real trucking jobs the V8-85 was still the engine of choice.

Some other changes made on the 1936 models included a switch from wire wheels to steel disc wheels. Hubcaps were changed to a different size and design. Modifications were noted in the louver design featured on the hood side panels, and the trim plates were moved from a center location to the front edges of these panels. The grille was also redesigned, especially on the commercial car models that were based on the passenger cars.

During the 1936 model year the Ford Motor Company celebrated a milestone when the 3 Millionth Ford Truck was produced. This truck, a panel model, all decked out with special trim in honor of the occasion, went on a national promotional tour to help sell more Ford trucks.

1937

Quite a few changes were noted on the 1937 car and truck offerings from Ford. Some involved design and appearances; others involved modifications to the driveline and in the chassis area too.

Starting with the engines, two versions of the V-8 were offered once again, the V8-60 and the V8-85. Both blocks were revised and redesigned to feature integrated, self-lubricating water pumps, revised valve guides, different front engine-mounting tabs and larger main-journal webs that now used insert bearings rather than the old poured babbitt type. The crankshaft was also improved and some modifications were made in the area of head design. Pistons got a domed crown and the combustion chambers were redesigned to match.

On the outside of the engine a new Stromberg 48 carburetor replaced the previously used Stromberg 97. An improved ignition system was employed to give better economy results, and the compression ratio was dropped to 6.12:1. The Ford engineers also brought out better steering and braking systems.

Though these mechanical updates were noteworthy, what made people stand up and notice these new Fords was their styling, which really set them apart from the competition as well as previous Fords. The new Fords featured new hoods, grilles, fenders, tops, trim and the like. They were changed all over. For instance, both the car line and the truck line featured new two-piece, vee'd windshields that replaced the old single-piece, flat windshield used before. The passenger-car-based vehicles now had their headlights integrated into the front fenders for a more streamlined look. Also adding to the streamlined look was a swept-back grille with complementary swept-back hood vents.

The commercial car line included a couple of new offerings to help Ford broaden its

---

1937 Options
4 speed transmission
Spyder stainless steel wheel covers
Right-hand sun visor
Right-hand windshield wiper
Defroster
Heater
Spotlight
Outside rearview mirror
Sliding back window for pickups
Radio
Clock
Whitewall tires
Deluxe Equipment Package: dual horns, dual sun visors, chrome-plated grille, chrome-plated windshield wipers, chrome-plated windshield frame, chrome-plated hood louver moldings
Two-tone paint
Special paint
Greyhound radiator ornament
Passenger seat (panel and sedan delivery)

The dual aspect of this 1937 Ford truck ad is appealing. Power and economy are the key words here as far as V-8 engines are concerned, the smaller one for economy, the larger one where power is needed. *Jerry Bougher*

A 1937 Ford pickup like this one isn't common at car and truck shows today. This one has been equipped with wide whitewalls that really dress it up.

market coverage. One new model was called a business coupe with pickup box. This was basically a five-window coupe body with a pickup bed mounted inside the trunk opening area. The bed was a bit shorter and narrower than a regular pickup box and was meant to carry supplies like what a traveling salesman might haul from town to town. This model was designed to appeal to salesmen, and it might have appealed to some but not enough to warrant listing it in the catalog after this model year.

The other new model was the light-duty stake bed, which was a real favorite with farmers. This model, and the similar platform unit, featured a flat hardwood body mounted atop a pedestal-type filler arrangement that placed the body more in line with loading docks to help facilitate loading and unloading chores.

The pickup model now featured a new bed that was about 4 in. longer than the unit used on the 1936 pickups. On the back side

of this box was a new tailgate with different hardware and an embossed V–8 emblem in the center. Front and rear bumpers were now standard equipment on the pickups as well as on the rest of the commercial car line.

The panel delivery came back again in both a half-ton rating and a full one-ton rating. These models featured an all-steel roof, dual rear doors, a spare tire side cover, a dome light and a hardwood cargo area floor. Ford offered a Suburban-type vehicle that was based on these panels. In essence it was a panel delivery vehicle with windows. Proctor-Keefe did the conversion work for Ford, and the result was available for order through any Ford dealer.

For the customer who wanted a car-based closed delivery the sedan delivery was again made available. It was offered in a base Standard model and a classier-looking Deluxe version. The Standard version outsold the fancier one by a 10:1 margin. The production figure for the Standard model was

7,841, and the Deluxe model sold around 707 units. The base prices were $585 for the Standard and $595 for the Deluxe.

The station wagon was also based on the car line again, and it could be had with a new all-glass option. Normally these station wagons came with glass in the windshield and glass in the two front doors, with the back window openings covered by canvas and isinglass covers. The all-glass option really cleaned up the looks of these cars and made the interior appear a lot lighter and airier. It also helped increase visibility, especially in inclement weather.

For those who wanted to mount their own bodies on Ford chassis the chassis and driveaway models were again available at a reduced cost.

As a safety feature all Ford-built products this year came with Safety Glass in the front windshield to cut down on injuries from glass during accidents.

Another change of note was Ford's National Economy Promotion Tour, which revolved around a "Scottie dog" theme. Quite a few of these trucks were built and painted in a special two-tone fashion for Ford dealers to help promote the V–8's economy. These traveling billboards probably helped to move Ford into first place in the truck sales world this year. Ford easily outdistanced Chevrolet and Dodge for truck sales leadership, especially in the light-duty ranks.

One last item involved the Marmon-Herrington four-wheel-drive Fords. Starting in late 1936 Marmon-Herrington offered such a conversion on all types of Ford commercial units ranging from the station wagon to the largest one-and-one-half-ton trucks. Few of them were originally converted, and today it might prove difficult to find one to restore.

Now here's a sharp looking restored 1938 Panel Delivery Van with wide whitewalls, trim rings and the like. This one is still used to haul goods for Lundrigan's Clothing.

A COE Ford stake from 1939.

1938-1939

No middle ground could be found when it came to the styling featured on the 1938 and 1939 Ford trucks. One either liked or disliked the look.

The major focal point concerned a redesigned large oval-type grille that some critics likened to a mouth sucking on a lemon. With a description like that you know this design was controversial in its time. But reflecting back from a fifty-year perspective one finds that it doesn't look all that bad, and after a while it tends to grow on one. In some respects the design even looks better than some of its contemporaries of fifty years ago.

These new Fords also featured redesigned hoods, front fenders and associated trim pieces, and in some cases a redesigned cab and running boards. The pickup model even received a new bed that featured all-steel, welded construction and a new tailgate that had three raised panels with the embossed

Ford V-8 logo occupying space in the center panel.

Over on the automobile side of the house Ford started a two-tier model policy. This approach offered Standard and Deluxe models that were now separated by different designs, different trim and different equipment considerations. The 1938 Standard models featured a design that was an updated version of the 1937 look, whereas the Deluxe model featured a look that was totally unique, especially in the front-end treatment. The Deluxe versions used a different hood and side-panel arrangement, as well as a different grille and hood-venting system. The Deluxe cars also came with larger and brighter wheel covers and other trim updates. From this point on, for the next couple of model years, one year's Deluxe design would appear as the following year's Standard version, while the Deluxe version would once again feature a redesign.

In the commercial car line of 1938, Ford's

two models that were based on its passenger cars, the sedan delivery and station wagon, at this point went down two separate paths. The sedan delivery models featured a design that was based on the Standard Ford passenger-car design, whereas the station wagon was now dressed out in Deluxe trim. Ford also started promoting the station wagons as both commercial cars and passenger cars. This type of dual-market strategy was a first because since 1929 Ford had always promoted these cars as commercial units. The new wagon models now featured glass in all window areas as standard equipment unless the customer specified side curtains in the back. They also featured lockable doors and windows, and a spare tire mounted inside rather than on the tailgate, as before.

Besides the new oval grille and revised front-end treatment the panel delivery models now had a new body with a more rounded top and a sloping back end.

In the engine compartment the V8–60 and V8–85 were still offered. The only change noted on them was a modification in spark-plug design, with 18 mm plugs now featured.

The stake and platform models were carried over and were again popular with farmers and light-duty carriers.

To broaden its market coverage a little further Ford offered a new line of one-ton models that were upgraded versions of its light-duty units. These one-tonners featured a 122 in. wheelbase, as compared with the 112 in. wheelbase found on the light-duty models. And instead of using a car frame, as the half-ton commercials did, the tonners used a heavier truck frame. In this new range of vehicles Ford offered an express pickup, panel delivery, stake and platform, as well as a drive-away chassis and chassis with cab.

Even with all these changes and additions 1938 was a disappointing year for Ford, especially as far as sales went. Ford was passed up by Chevrolet, which took the lead and never relinquished it for thirty years or so.

In spite of these setbacks Ford forged on with quite a few changes that made their debut on its 1939 commercial car line.

Once again Ford's passenger car line was split up into the two-tier Standard and Deluxe models. The Standard models used the design that was featured on the 1938 Deluxe, whereas the Deluxe models featured a new design in their grille and hood. The Deluxe version again came with fancier trim, as it had the previous year.

The station wagon model was available in Standard or Deluxe car trim. The upper models featured genuine leather upholstery, plated carriage bolts on the exterior, a chrome windshield molding and larger fancier-looking wheel covers. The Standard model came with an interior that was done up in an artificial leather, and its trim was rather muted as compared with that of the fancier Deluxe. The Standard came in a Wren Tan color for the sheet metal, and the Deluxe was painted a Maroon color unless the customer specified a different color.

For the sedan delivery buyer only one body style was available and that was of the Standard form. Though it wasn't as flashy as, say, a Deluxe station wagon, it was nicely fitted out with dual windshield wipers, a fully lined and insulated interior, and other amenities. It was one classy-looking delivery car for a base price of $685 when powered by a V8–85. Nowadays it's a hard one to find, since Ford built only 2,800 of them back in 1939.

Ford still offered the panel delivery, and it looked pretty much the same as the 1938 model. Ford did add some more insulation in the lower body area to help seal this body better and to help quiet it down some.

Between the half-ton commercial car line and the one-ton truck line Ford added a new group of vehicles that it called its three-quarter-ton series. These vehicles used the same wheelbases as the tonners, set at 122 in. rather than the 112 in. of the half-ton vehicles. In this new line Ford offered express pickup, panel delivery, platform and stake models. These three-quarter-ton vehicles used the same engines and transmissions that the half-ton vehicles used.

If one needed a larger vehicle than the new three-quarter-ton trucks Ford still offered its Tonner Series in the same models as the lower-ranked three-quarter-tons. Power, in standard equipment form, was the same as for the two lower series, but if more power was needed Ford offered a new 239 ci V–8 as an extracost option in this range of vehicles. That 239 ci V–8 carried the same horsepower rating as the new Mercury car, 95 hp.

The best news for 1939 from a safety standpoint was that all Ford vehicles now featured hydraulic brakes. Now Ford could say its vehicles could stop as well as any other. Better brakes, more economy, more models, more options and more power on tap for some Ford models: Ford had all the bases covered when it came to offering light-duty commercial vehicles that embraced a wide market range.

A fully equipped Pennsylvania Bell System Telephone truck from 1939. *Applegate & Applegate*

Chapter 5

1940–1947
High Style Trucks

Many people consider the 1940 models to be the most beautiful Fords ever produced, which might explain why they have always been so popular, both when they were new and every year since then. Starting off with the trucks this time around, Ford carried over all the models that were available in 1939 in light-, medium- and heavy-duty forms—in half-, three-quarter- and one-ton ratings.

The most pleasing aspect of these new Fords was the styling cues that were taken

This 1940 Ford woodie Deluxe station wagon is all original except for a couple of bullet holes in the hood. Its present owner received it from his grandfather, who originally purchased the car in 1940.

directly from Ford's automobile line. These features included a restyled hood, sealed-beam headlights, and a grille that was similar to the one on the 1939 Ford Deluxe car and the 1940 Ford Standard car model. Ford's trucks also featured an all-new, revamped cab, whose major styling focal point was a single, one-piece, stamped-steel front panel that combined the cowl, firewall, windshield frame and top. Heretofore these pieces were all separate and welded together to produce a single unit. By using this one-piece affair Ford did away with seams, making for a simpler assembly procedure, which really helped out on the assembly line. This new design also featured cowl-mounted windshield wipers; before 1940 wipers were mounted above the windshield on the front part of the top panel.

On the inside Ford redesigned the instrument cluster into a single unit in a rectangular shape just like the one it used in its passenger cars. It also added more coils inside the seat to make it more comfortable. Another carlike feature was a two-spoke steering wheel.

Once again the station wagon models were offered in Standard or Deluxe passenger-car trim. Both models used a body that was redesigned, especially in the rear-door area where it now featured doors that opened toward the back rather than toward the front. Both the wood framing used and the paneling were also changed a bit. On the inside the Deluxe models used genuine

A 1940 Ford pickup fully equipped with period accessories like wide whitewalls, chrome head- light rings, grille guard and foglights. *Elliott Kahn*

leather coverings, whereas the Standard version had to make do with artificial-leather coverings. On both models the spare tire was moved back outside again and mounted on the tailgate. Ford promoted these cars again as both passenger vehicles and commercial vehicles.

In a turnabout situation the sedan delivery was available only in Deluxe car trim rather than in the Standard car guise it employed in 1939. These closed-car deliveries were outfitted in an upscale fashion, featuring a fully lined interior, a clock, dual sun visors, dual ashtrays, a leather seat covering or coverings, and a three-speed manual transmission with a column-mounted shift lever. These sedan deliveries were popular, with sales topping out around 4,900 units, a good 2,100 above what Ford sold in 1939.

As far as engines go, in the commercial car line of half-ton and three-quarter-ton models the V8–60 and V8–85 were carried over.

The 239 ci 95 hp V–8 was also used in some cars and pickup trucks.

The 1941 Ford offerings mirrored what was available to the buyer in the 1940 model year. The pickup, panel delivery, stake, platform and chassis models all used the same styling as similar 1940 units. The sedan delivery and the station wagon featured the looks of the redesigned 1941 Ford passenger car line. The sedan delivery went back to Standard car trim, and the station wagons were available in Deluxe and Super Deluxe forms.

Though the 1941 truck models looked the same as the 1940 versions on the inside and outside, under the hood things were quite a bit different. The 221 ci V–8 started out with an 85 hp rating at the beginning of the model year, but that rating was boosted to 90 hp by midyear. As before, the 239 ci V–8 rated at 95 hp was still available as an extra-cost

53

A 1940 Ford panel delivery truck. This promotional photograph shows a driver carrying a
load of groceries to someone's door. *Applegate
& Applegate*

Custom wheels and a lowering job turned this
1940 Ford pickup into a neat street rod.

option on a special order basis in the light-duty trucks.

The little V8-60 was dropped at the end of the 1940 model year, and in its place Ford offered two economy engines. One was a 119 ci inline four-cylinder engine that Ford pulled from its 9N tractor program. This little workhorse put out a miserly 30 hp and economy figures that were little better than those of the V8-60 it replaced.

For people who needed a little extra power with their economy engines Ford offered a newly designed inline L-head six-cylinder engine that displaced 226 ci. This engine put out 90 hp at 3200 rpm versus the 90 hp at 3800 rpm put out by the 221 ci V-8. Though the six-cylinder and V-8 engines were rated the same in horsepower, they differed quite a bit in torque ratings: the 226 ci six-cylinder produced 180 lb-ft at 1200 rpm, and the 221 ci V-8 produced 150 lb-ft at 2200 rpm. In layman's terms the six had more muscle at 1000 fewer rpm, which meant it pulled better with less strain—which translated into better economy figures.

Dropping the four-cylinder powerplant into the Ford truck chassis didn't pose too much of a problem because the four-cylinder was basically the same length as the V-8. However, the six-cylinder engine was a far different story. Since the inline six was longer than the V-8, dropping it into this engine compartment opened up a real can of worms for the Ford engineers. To get around this problem the Ford engineering staff used a set of frame extenders that allowed the radiator to be moved forward in the chassis to provide the needed clearance. They also came up with a new set of engine mounts and pads for the six, and revised the

1940–1941 Options
Engines
   239 ci 95 hp V-8
   226 ci 90 hp 6 cylinder (1941)
   119 ci 30 hp 4 cylinder (1941)
4 speed transmission
Plated rear bumper
Passenger seat (panel and sedan delivery)
Spare tire
Spotlight
Radio
Engine governor
Foglights
Bumper guards
Right-side sun visor
Locking gas cap
Sliding rear window
Right-side windshield wiper
Whitewall tires
Heavy-duty tires
Heavy-duty 11 in. clutch
Foam padded seat
Heater
Fender skirts
Wheel trim rings
Mirrors
Grille guard
Grille winter cover
Bumper wing tips
Taillamps
Oil filters
Oil bath air cleaner
Overdrive transmissions
Spare tire carriers
Deluxe Trim Packages
Special paint
Two-tone paint

A 1940 Ford Deluxe sedan delivery. This one has been slightly modified.

This 1941 Ford pickup has been in the same family since new.

This 1941 Ford half-ton pickup features red pin-stripes and red wheels. The exterior color is a medium green.

When I was much younger, I went to an amusement park where for a nickel I could pick up a photo card like this one from an arcade machine. The truck pictured here is a customized 1940 Ford from the mid-1950s.

inner fender panels for added room. The throttle and choke mechanisms for this purpose were actuated by cables rather than rods, as used in V-8 applications. Also, the battery box tray in the six-cylinder-equipped trucks was moved over to the other side of the compartment for clearance. When the engineers were done with all these modifications the six-cylinder engines looked as if they were designed to fit right into this chassis, rather than the other way around. Here, necessity was indeed the mother of invention.

Since Ford offered other engines this year in addition to the V-8, all traces of V-8 logos and emblems were removed from the body and hubcaps found on 1941 trucks. Instead a simple Ford nameplate or logo was used.

The handsome styling of the 1940-1941 Fords set them apart from their contemporaries. It's a style that has withstood the test of time and will continue to do so for generations to come.

1942

The dark clouds of war were moving ever closer to US shores in the fall of 1941 when the Ford Motor Company released its extensively reworked 1942 models. Judging by all the changes that made their debut on these models and how much promise they held for

Front-end details of this 1940 Ford pickup show the grille hood trim and headlight rims that have been chromed like those used on the Deluxe series of Ford cars for that year.

success, it must have been hard to imagine that in a few months all would be for naught because the factories would have to shut down to convert over to military production. Nevertheless, the plug was put in civilian, nonessential production in February of 1942, a couple of months after the Japanese attacked Pearl Harbor on December 7, 1941.

Nowhere was change more evident in the 1942 models than in the half-ton vehicles, which still included pickup, panel delivery, stake, platform and chassis models. Starting

There are always a lot of interesting trucks at the American Truck Historical Society meets. This is a 1941 Ford pickup that looked sharp in red with wide whitewalls.

at the bottom and working our way up we find that the half-ton models now featured a full truck frame rather than the modified car frames they used before. These frames were of a ladder-type construction featuring four strong cross-members. The frame rails were placed 34 in. apart, just as they were in the frames used on larger trucks.

On the front of these frames Ford replaced the single-transverse-spring arrangement with a straight beam front axle that was suspended by a pair of longitudinal leaf springs. A new transverse steering tie rod and drag-link arrangement provided a better steering system. A set of heavy-duty shocks helped to dampen out some of the jolts that were transmitted up from the pavement through the axles.

On the back side of the frames a set of semi-elliptic longitudinal leaf springs replaced the single transverse spring that was

used before. The old torque-tube and radius-rod rear end was replaced by a new Hotchkiss design. Shock absorbers were available at extra cost if so desired.

Other changes noted on the underside of these new trucks were a new exhaust system, engine and transmission mounts, and a new wheelbase length of 114 in., up from the 112 in. wheelbase used before. A 114 in. wheelbase was also featured on Ford's passenger cars for 1942.

Moving into the engine compartment we find that Ford once again offered three choices with its four-cylinder, six-cylinder and V-8 engines. The four-cylinder modified tractor engine still displaced 119.7 ci and still put out 30 hp at 2800 rpm. It featured a 3.19 in. bore and a 3.75 in. stroke. Its compression ratio stood at 6.0:1, so it could run on just about any type or quality of gasoline.

Next on the agenda was the six-cylinder

This 1941 Ford Motor Company promotional photo shows a pre-production pickup model that is equipped with a side-mounted spare tire, black wheels and a single-tone paint finish. *Ford Motor Company*

powerplant that was rated at 90 hp at 3800 rpm. This engine featured a 3.3 in. bore and a 4.4 in. stroke for a grand total of 226 ci. Its strongest point again was its torque rating of 180 lb-ft at 1200 rpm. This was a lot of torque for an engine of that size, and because it was so torquey Ford specified that a 10 in. clutch be used behind it. By comparison, in standard equipment form the four and the 221 ci V–8 both used 9 in. clutch discs.

Besides the 221 in. V–8 Ford still offered the 239 ci V–8 as an option. This engine was now rated at 100 hp.

Behind the V–8s and the six, Ford installed three-speed truck transmissions as standard equipment. Behind the four a four-speed was fitted because this little engine needed

POWER AND APPEARANCE AT A PRICE *You'll like!*

A 1941 Ford truck promotional postcard.

an extra gear because it was down in power. As extra-cost options for the V–8s and the six, Ford had heavy-duty three-speed transmissions or four-speed transmissions available. Heavy-duty clutches were available too.

Further changes were made in the engine compartment, and these involved a new design for the radiator and new rubber insulated radiator supports. On the engine itself, the fan, related pulleys and belts were all relocated to provide for better cooling.

Just as many changes were made on the outside of these vehicles as on the underside and in the engine compartment. The cabs were the same ones used in 1941, but front-end pieces like the hood, fenders, grille and bumpers were all changed. The focal point that brought all these divergent elements together was the grille frontal piece. This large flat piece held the headlights and a new vertical-bar grille. In the United States these grilles were called "waterfalls"; in some parts of the world they were called "jail-house" grilles because of the similarity noted in the bar design. In any event this type of new grille made it easy to identify this type of new Ford.

In 1941 the US Postal Service had a few Ford mail trucks in its fleet. They were painted dark green with black fenders. *Applegate & Applegate*

A rare 1942 Ford panel delivery truck. Few were built as the assembly lines were shut down to convert to war production. *Applegate & Applegate*

Though the hood didn't look like it, it was the same unit used on the 1940 and 1941 Ford trucks. What made it look different was the hood trim pieces and new vent-port design featured on the hood sides. The fenders now were two-piece affairs on the front that were somewhat wider and a little flatter on the top than what was used before. These fenders featured a series of compound curves, so it was probably easier for Ford to bolt two stampings together rather than try to stamp out such a complex unit in a single piece of steel.

On the back side of the cab the pickup's box was a new unit that was a little longer and wider than the model used on the 1938–1941 trucks.

On the inside a new instrument panel gauge cluster was fitted, as was a revamped seat.

Because of its new truck-style frame the panel delivery truck featured an extra 3 in. of inside body height, and once again the cargo-area walls were protected from cargo shift by steel lower panels and hardwood vertical posts. The panel delivery, as well as the sedan delivery, used a 17 gallon fuel tank, whereas the other half-ton models used 19 gallon tanks.

Dashboard details on a 1941 Ford pickup show a simple instrument cluster grouped in a rectangular panel. Note the starter switch mounted on the left side.

One of Ford's assembly lines in 1942 with Jeeps going through final assembly tests before being driven off the line. *Ford Motor Company*

In 1942, Ford built quite a few Jeeps like this restored field command unit complete with rope, shovels and a trailer in tow.

Like the passenger-car models it was based on, the sedan delivery featured a new look for 1942. These models featured the Super Deluxe passenger-car treatment, as did the station wagons. Both the sedan delivery and the station wagon featured concealed running boards that gave them a more modern look. The station wagon models also featured roll-up windows in the back as well as in the doors. Previously the back windows were of the sliding type.

For the half-ton models, sedan deliveries and station wagons, a 6.00x16 four-ply tire in black or whitewall was called for in the specifications. The three-quarter-ton and one-ton trucks used 6.00x16 six-ply tires, which could also be fitted on the half-ton models for an additional charge.

The 1942 model year should have been one of Ford's best with all the changed vehicles it brought to the marketplace. However, owing to unforeseen circumstances, the pro-

duction run was cut short so that Ford could concentrate on building war machinery to defeat the Axis powers. Where once proud cars and trucks had been built, now jeeps, bombers and tanks were being assembled.

Owing to the shortened production run 1942 vehicles are rare today. It's too bad because Ford made some great vehicles during this rather short period of time.

1945–1947

Tanks, bombers, jeeps, amphibious vehicles, gliders and the like—thousands of them—rolled off the Ford assembly lines during the years of World War II. Interspersed with these weapons of war were more common vehicles of commerce like tractors, buses, trucks and even a few sedans to help on both the war front and the home front.

With all this plant activity going on at such a feverish pace Ford's workers were con-

A rare 1942 Ford sedan delivery.

stantly kept on their toes. So when the need for machines of war started to wane in early 1945 it didn't take too long to convert over from military to civilian production. Since getting American businesses back on track was considered to be of prime importance at this time, production of commercial vehicles was given the nod over production of regular passenger vehicles at first. Thus renewed Ford civilian truck production preceded car production by two months or so.

One of the first Ford civilian trucks down those assembly lines was a special pickup model that turned out to be a milestone vehicle in Ford Motor Company history. This Village Green truck with Tacoma Cream accents was the 31 millionth Ford vehicle produced since the company was formed back in 1903.

This 1945 model and others like it looked pretty much the same as the last civilian trucks produced before the plug was pulled in 1942. As a matter of fact, somebody seeing that truck rolling off the line in May of 1945 might have thought that time had

Hood side details showing Tacoma Cream painted trim and Ford script as used from 1942–1947.

The 1946 Ford Super Deluxe station wagon was one of the most expensive Fords offered that year.

This Railway Express Agency truck is an example of one of Ford's chassis and cowl models produced during the 1940s. This particular example is used as a hot-air balloon chase vehicle now.

A California artist uses this rare 1947 sedan delivery to promote her business. Some of her artwork can be seen displayed on this vehicle's signboards.

stood still between it and the 1942 models that preceded it. They shared styling, trim and, for the most part, equipment. But some changes were made to the new trucks under the skin, and these modifications made the new trucks a little bit better than those that came before.

One of those changes revolved around the 239 ci 100 hp V-8. This was the only power-plant available at the start of production. New features found on this engine included a set of redesigned aluminum pistons, silver-alloy bearings, an improved ignition system, a larger oil pump and a pressurized cooling system. These modifications helped the engines to run smoother and cooler, and to last a lot longer.

Other changes seen on these trucks included wider frame rails, metal frames around the cab's window glass and a new steering-box mounting point.

Though Ford and the other manufactur-ers were now free to produce civilian vehi-cles, steel and other material shortages kept production limited for most of this model year. Because of these shortages some 1942 models didn't make the cut for 1945—mod-els like Ford's three-quarter-ton series of vehicles and sedan deliveries. Panel deliver-ies were in short supply also because Ford was concentrating its efforts on building pickups, stakes, cab-and-chassis models, and school buses.

Things got a little better for the 1946 model year because with the surrender of the Japanese World War II finally came to an end. With the war now a memory more raw materials used in the production of cars and trucks became available for the manufactur-ers' use. The manufacturers in turn took advantage of the situation by building more vehicles and a wider variety of them.

This original-condition 1947 Ford sedan delivery was purchased in the early 1970s from the original owners, who used it to deliver groceries from their store. *Rick Louderbough*

In Ford's light-duty truck line, formerly called its commercial car series, the sedan delivery came back to join the pickup, as did the panel delivery.

The sedan delivery featured new styling that was again taken from the Deluxe passenger-car series, making this a handsome delivery vehicle. Once again the station wagon was based on the Super Deluxe car series, though now it was promoted more as a regular passenger car and less as a commercial vehicle.

Self-centering brakes became standard equipment on both cars and light-duty trucks, and the 1946 light-duty trucks received carlike hubcaps. The only color available on the 1945 trucks was Village Green, but the 1946 and 1947 trucks were available in colors like Moonstone Gray, Modern Blue, Vermillion (red), Greenfield Green and Black. These colors were highlighted with trim pieces painted in Tacoma Cream. The station wagon and sedan deliveries were available in these colors as well as Navy Blue, Botsford Blue Green, Dynamic Maroon, Willow Green and Dark Slate Gray Metallic.

Prices for Ford's light-duty commercial vehicles ranged from a low of $852 for a cowl-and-chassis model to a high of $1,270 for a one-ton stake. The sedan delivery and the panel delivery were priced within $3 of each other at $1,186 and $1,189 respectively.

Engine availability in 1946 included the 239 ci V-8 and the 226 ci six. The difference in price between the two amounted to only $15. The 226 ci six was the standard powerplant, with the V-8 costing extra. Ford started promoting the six over the V-8 at this end of the market, figuring that sixes used here freed up that many more V-8s for use in larger trucks. And besides, the six gave better economy numbers than the V-8, which appealed to cost-conscious buyers back then.

Things looked still better for Ford and the market overall in the 1947 model year. A seller's market still existed, and with supplies of steel, rubber and glass growing daily, production numbers increased by a large amount. By the end of the model year Ford light-duty truck sales passed the 91,400 unit mark—a total that was good when one considers that Ford's chief competitor, Chevrolet, had released a restyled line of trucks in 1947.

Ford's response to Chevrolet was a line of extensively restyled trucks that would make their debut in the 1948 model year. These trucks would look every bit as modern as the Chevys and Dodges they would compete against later on.

AAA Plumbing and Solar has a distinctive service truck, a vintage Ford panel delivery.

Chapter 6

1948–1952 Bonus Built Trucks

★★★★	1948–1950 F–1 pickup, panel, stake
★★★	1948–1952 Marmon-Herrington all-wheel-drive
★★★	1948–1952 F–2 pickup, stake
★★	1948–1952 F–3 pickup, stake
★★	1948–1952 Chassis, chassis cowl
★★★★	1951–1952 F–1 pickup, panel, stake
★★★	1952 Courier sedan delivery

The main reason Ford didn't spend any money changing anything on its 1947 models was that all its money was going into development work on a totally revised line of trucks for 1948. Ford knew that to compete successfully in the truck market after the seller's market subsided in the late forties it would have to come up with something special to attract buyers and keep them in the Ford fold. These new trucks would have to be more special than any Fords that preceded them and better than the competi-

The Bonus Built Ford F–1 panels built in 1948–1952 are good-looking commercial vehicles in their own right. If you like your vehicles with a little more glitter you might want to find a 1950 Mercury panel like the one pictured here.

We can tell that this panel delivery is a late 1948 or 1949 model by its argent-silver-finished grille bars and backplate panel. *Don Bunn*

tion. Ford spent a lot of money, time and effort to reach this goal, and reach it, it did, with its Bonus Built truck line, which made its debut in January of 1948.

Bonus Built, as the name implied, offered more for the money, or "more truck for the buck." The "more," in this instance, included a more stylish cab, a roomier cab, more standard equipment, more options, and a wider range of models from a half-ton pickup to a three-ton semitractor, in conventional or cab-over-engine form.

In light-duty guise these Bonus Built trucks were available in three versions, with model designations of F–1, F–2 and F–3. The F–1 series covered half-ton rated vehicles, the F–2 series covered a reintroduced three-quarter-ton range and the F–3 series covered vehicles with a one-ton rating.

The primary focus on these new trucks revolved around their new cabs, which were

Bonus Built Ford trucks of the 1948–1952 period are easy vehicles to customize. This one has custom wheels and tires, tarp, custom tailgate and modern mirrors.

The 1948–1952 rear tailgate Ford script.

A restored 1950 F–1 pickup.

a full 7 in. wider, 3 in. longer and 3 in. taller than the cabs they replaced, making them larger, roomier and more comfortable than what was offered before. The 3 in. longer doors made entry and exit quite a bit easier. As added bonuses, these cabs featured new instrument panels and a wider, more comfortable seat. They also featured a new larger one-piece windshield and a larger rear window as well.

Ford also spent considerable sums to redo the front-end clips on these trucks. These clips featured redesigned flatter and wider hoods, wider two-piece fenders and a new recessed grille panel. The hood now used vent ports on its front as well as on its sides. The hood-release latch was cleverly designed to form a piece of trim that was fitted into the front vent ports. A series of five horizontal bars made up the grille, rather than the vertical motif that was used before. These bars were chromed at the beginning of the model year and painted argent silver toward the end of the model year. A tan-painted backing plate was placed behind the grille bars at first, but this was also changed to a silver color during the model year. The parking lights were located on the ends of the top grille bar.

Other changes found on these trucks included trim updates and the moving of the spare tire back underneath the body on the pickup, stake and platform models.

Though they looked all-new up top, everything on the bottom side was carried over from the 1947 model year.

Changes on the 1949 models were for the most part minimal in nature, revolving mostly around paint color choices. The horizontal grille bars and backing plates were painted silver starting with the late 1948 models, and the wheels on light-duty trucks were painted body color rather than black, as they were on the 1948 models.

A new model joined the 1949 Ford light-duty line under the F–3 series. This was a walk-in delivery vehicle called the parcel delivery. Ford offered it with a front-end piece that included a grille, bumper, cowl and windshield arrangement, to which a customer added his or her own aftermarket-supplied body. This model was meant to be a companion to the half-ton panel but allowed the customer to carry a larger, bulkier payload, thanks to the increased cargo area.

Two F-1 pickups. The one on the left is a 1948, while the one on the right is a 1950.

For 1950 the F-1 panel delivery van wasn't changed from what was offered in 1949, as you can see in this promotional photograph. *Don Bunn*

A 1952 5 Star cab instrument panel detail. The speedometer on the right side reads to 90 mph. Oil-pressure, fuel, water-temperature and battery gauges are all grouped together in a single pod on the left.

Some 1952 Ford F-1 pickups made pretty good race trucks as this *Farm Hand* D/Gasser shows. This particular truck terrorized Midwest dragstrips in the mid-1960s. *John Jacobsen collection*

Changes seen on the 1950 models were even less substantial than those seen on the 1949 trucks. The only modifications involved some color choices and the moving of the shift lever from the floor to the steering column on the F-1 trucks—a move that made these cabs more comfortable, especially if three adults were riding in the cab.

For most people, telling the 1948, 1949 and 1950 Ford trucks apart is rather difficult, since no noteworthy changes existed to help differentiate between them. This ar-

1948–1952 Production

Year	Total
1948	108,006
1949	104,803
1950	148,956
1951	117,414
1952	145,201

1948–1952 Options

Transmissions
   Heavy-duty 3 speed manual
   Heavy-duty 4 speed manual
   Overdrive (Courier 1952)
4.09:1 rear axle (1951–52)
4.27:1 rear axle (standard on some models)
11 in. clutch
Spiralounge bucket seat (panel)
Heavy-duty radiator
Heavy-duty battery
MagicAire heater and defroster
Recirculating heater and defroster
Radio
Right-hand sun visor
Seat covers
Hi-Way horns
Right-hand windshield wiper
Sealed beam spotlight
Road lamps
Fire extinguisher
Reflector and flare set
See Clear windshield washer
Tool kit
Front tow hooks
Cigar lighter
Leather-covered armrests
Mirrors
Tires
   7.00x16 in.
   7.50x16 in.
   7.50x17 in. (F-350)
   Whitewalls
Radiator overflow tank
Five Star Extra Package (1951–52)
Grille guard
Right rear taillight
Rear bumper
Windshield visor

Hood front-end details on 1952 F Series trucks included *Ford* letters on the upper grille panel and hood vent ports. The stylized medallion in the hood front trim piece indicates this truck has a six-cylinder engine under its hood. The V–8 equipped trucks wore V–8 emblems.

rangement may have worked for a while, but to keep sales momentum up some changes had to be made in the Bonus Built trucks to keep the buyers coming back.

Those changes came with the 1951 models that featured the Five Star cab and the Five Star Extra cab. The former was an updated standard cab offering; the latter was strictly deluxe all the way. The Five Star cab offered three-way ventilation, an adjustable seat, dual windshield wipers, a driver's-side visor, a dispatch box and an ashtray. To that package the Five Star Extra cab added such niceties as foam padding in the seat; a headliner covering a fiberglass and wool insulating pad; extra sound-deadening material in the doors, on the floor and on the rear cab panel; brightmetal finish trim pieces around the windshield and vent windows; and some additional brightmetal trim pieces on the hood. An argent finish was applied to the grille bar, and a two-tone upholstery cover was used on the seat. Other extras included locks on both doors and the dispatch box, armrests on both doors, a dome light and twin horns.

The 1951 models also featured a new grille bar that consisted of a series of three dagmar orbs, revamped fenders and a bumper design change.

The 1951 models also featured some new items under the hood. The 1951 version of the 239 ci V–8 used new water pumps, fan, bellhousing, manifolds, generator, carburetor, oil pump, valves, clutch, flywheel and a

For 1952 Ford revamped its hood side trim by adding a round disk to the chrome side spear. The model designation—F-1, F-2 or F-3—was put in the center of this disk.

This 1952 F-1 model is of the Standard cab variety that Ford called the 5 Star. It's been painted to look like new in its factory green paint with cream-colored wheels, grille and hood front trim piece.

This 1952 F-1 5 Star cab model has a six-cylinder engine under the hood. The eight-cylinder models had a V-8 emblem on the hood front trim piece.

host of other refinements. Ford also promoted a new device on these engines that it called a Power Pilot. This was basically a vacuum line that connected the carburetor with the distributor. This device helped to advance the distributor spark by means of a vacuum signal that matched the spark to the demands of the engine load, thus improving economy.

Big news on the 1952 Bonus Built front involved a major redesign for the six-cylinder engine. Gone was the flathead 226 cubic incher, replaced by a smaller, more modern, more powerful overhead valve engine that displaced 215 ci. Though smaller by 11 ci, this engine actually put out an additional 6 hp, with 101 hp versus 95 hp. To compensate for this power increase in the six the V–8 was boosted an extra 6 hp, so it was now rated at 106 hp.

Another bit of good news for 1952 was the return of a sedan delivery vehicle to the Ford commercial line. This model was now called the Courier Custom sedan delivery and was based on the new two-door ranch wagon station wagon. These models were available in ten complementary exterior colors. On the inside the seat or seats were covered in a vinyl material and gray-colored Masonite interior panels were used.

Regular 1952 changes seen on the light-duty trucks included the use of a white-painted grille and hood front trim pieces, the revamping of side trim (changing trim bars and adding discs to show model designations) and the addition of Ford lettering on the grille upper plate surround.

Over the course of five model years, 1948 through 1952, the Bonus Built light-duty models certainly got the job done for Ford. More than 624,000 of them rolled off the assembly lines to an appreciative audience.

This 1952 5 Star Extra Cab pickup has been personalized by it's owner with fender-mounted turn signal lamps, a spotlight, whitewall tires and rain deflectors.

Chapter 7

1953–1956 Economy Line Trucks

★★★★	1953–1956 Courier sedan delivery
★★★★	1953–1955 F–100 pickup, panel, stake
★★★	1953–1956 F–250 pickup, stake
★★★	1953–1956 F–350 pickup, stake
★★	1953–1956 Chassis, chassis cowl, chassis windshield
★★	1953–1956 Parcel delivery
★★★	1953–1956 Marmon-Herrington all-wheel-drive
★★★★	1956 F–100 pickup, panel, stake
★★★★	1956 F–100 Custom Cab pickup, panel
★★★★★	1956 F–100 Custom Cab pickup, big back window option

The Ford Motor Company faced a major dilemma in the early fifties. This dilemma revolved around the problem of finding a worthy successor to its highly successful Bonus Built trucks of the 1948–1952 period. Ford was facing a rather big job to improve itself and its products in this type of situa-

In the 1950s Ford dealers used promotional postcards like this one, which showed a 1953 F–100 panel, to mail out to prospects.

They're Here!

**GREATEST FORD TRUCKS
EVER BUILT FOR
FARM WORK**

Availability of equipment, accessories
and trim as illustrated is dependent
on material supply conditions.

FARMERS' FAVORITE—
the Ford F-100 Pickup—has
new 6½-ft. pickup box with
new, rigid, clamp-tight tailgate.

"Fifty Years
Forward
on the
American
Road!"

Completely New for '53...
FORD *ECONOMY* TRUCKS

NEW *TIMESAVING* FEATURES GET JOBS DONE FAST!

Ford *Economy* Trucks for '53 are completely new from the tires up! New cabs, new chassis, new power, new transmissions . . . designed to save time, provide quick, economical transportation in every kind of farm work. New Ford Truck *timesaving features* GET JOBS DONE FAST . . . at still *lower* cost!

NEW "DRIVERIZED" CABS
cut driver fatigue!

New one-piece curved windshield, 55% bigger! Wider seat, with new *shock absorber*. Larger door opening, pushbutton handles.

NEW SPRINGS! NEW BRAKES!
New features throughout!

Longer springs for easier ride, longer life! New, powerful, self-energizing brakes designed for safer, surer stopping with lighter pedal pressures. New frames! New axles!

NEW TRANSMISSIONS,
widest choice in truck history!

Fordomatic Drive or Overdrive available in ½-tonners (extra cost). Synchro-Silent transmissions throughout eliminate "double clutching." Steering column shift standard with all 3-speed transmissions.

NEW SHORTER TURNING
for timesaving maneuverability!

New, wider tread gives greater steering angle, more stability. New set-back front axle shortens wheelbase for better weight distribution and improved ride control under all operating conditions.

NEW LOW-FRICTION POWER!
Choice of 5 engines . . . V-8 or Six!

Overhead valve, 101-h.p. *Cost Clipper* Six cuts friction "power waste,"saves gas. Famous 106-h.p. Truck V-8, 112-h.p. Big Six and LOW-FRICTION overhead valve 145- and 155-h.p. *Cargo King* V-8's!

This ad shows the new 1953 Ford trucks. Note the "50th Anniversary" medallion being displayed in this ad. *Michael MacSems collection*

Not too many 1953 F-100 pickups were equipped with factory radios like the one here. In cases where a customer wanted a radio, the radio was installed in the dashboard and the speaker was mounted overhead above the windshield.

tion. It was a goal it knew it couldn't take lightly, so to do the best job possible it put its best engineers on the project and made a serious commitment of time, money, effort and workers to see the program through to completion. Over the course of two and a half years it would spend more than $30 million and untold work hours to bring the most extensively revamped Ford product line to market for the 1953 model year.

Ford historians already know that 1953 was a milestone year, for during it the company celebrated its golden anniversary—fifty years of doing business since Henry Ford started the company back in 1903.

The Ford passenger-car line had made its debut in 1952 with an all-new look, so it was only slated for a mild redo for 1953. This was hardly something for the company to cele-brate, but in honor of the occasion Ford products received a special commemorative 50th anniversary horn button. This program was not quite up to the level of show-case status; for that the Ford people would turn to their new, redesigned economy line of trucks, which bowed on March 13, 1953.

These trucks were stunning, with lines that really set them apart from their con-temporaries. Their classic lines were appeal-ing to the eye and timeless in scope—so much so that even today their design is appreciated more than that of any other Ford truck vehicles that come to mind.

These new trucks embodied several changes in addition to their styling, but we'll concentrate on that styling to begin with. First, they featured new, rather bulbous

Marmon-Herrington four-wheel-drive Ford trucks in the early 1950s wore a tag like this on their hoodsides. *Kenny Campbell*

Five Star Extra Package

All models
Dome light with door switches
Deluxe door trim
Dual horns
Foam rubber seat padding
Vinyl-and-mohair combination seat cover
Extra sound insulation
Cigarette lighter
Distinctive hood trim pieces
Headlining

Panel trucks
Everything listed above plus everything
  listed below
Auxiliary passenger seat with matching
  two-tone seat upholstery
Heavy Masonite side paneling
Perforated headlining covering a fiberglass
  and wool insulating pad
Matching sun visors (1952)
Locks on all doors and glovebox (1952)

1953–1956 Production

Model	Total
1953	
F–100	133,439
F–250	28,599
F–350	15,773
P–350	2,504
Courier	10,575
Total	190,890
1954	
F–100	117,587
F–250	25,642
F–350	13,887
P–350	2,383
Courier	6,404
Total	165,903
1955	
F–100	145,162
F–250	29,174
F–350	17,507
P–350	3,825
Courier	7,754
Total	203,422
1956	
F–100	188,836
F–250	36,389
F–350	24,620
P–350	6,054
Courier	8,757
Total	264,656
Grand total	824,871

The 1953–1955 Deluxe F Series cab. Note the
dual sun visors, two-tone seat cover and special
door panel trim. *Don Bunn collection*

An original 1955 F-100 promotional postcard.

This factory photo shows a 1956 F-100 Custom cab model. This truck is equipped with a V-8, Ford-O-Matic transmission, and the two-tone paint option. *Don Bunn collection*

front fenders that were quite a bit different than the fenders used before. Their hoods were flatter and quite a bit wider, and they also featured a redesigned grille cavity and a wider grille bar to boot. The new redesigned cabs were wider, longer and taller, and incorporated a lot more glass area.

Though the exterior of these trucks was the first item noticed, Ford spent a fair amount of development time improving the environment of the cab. It strived to achieve a cab more suited to the driver, figuring that if the driver and passengers were more comfortable they could be more productive. To achieve this goal the Ford interior engineers used a set of mannequins to properly locate all the elements needed to produce a more comfortable cab. Through this research they came up with a wider seat, a different angle for the steering column and steering wheel, and the centralized grouping of gauges and control knobs in front of the driver. Though they may not have realized it at the time, this attention to detail later became a science known as ergonomics, which is still called upon to produce similar results.

Mechanical changes were kept to a minimum, but one change that helped make these new Ford trucks somewhat easier to handle was their new, set-back front axle. This change alone allowed more weight to be carried on the front axle, making for a better balance between the front and back. This setup also allowed for a shorter turning

A 1955 Deluxe pickup in a two-tone finish is compared to a 1954 model in this factory photograph. Note that the 1955 is powered by a V-8 and the 1954 grille star tells us it is powered by a six-cylinder engine. *Ford Motor Company*

A personalized 1956 Ford F-100 pickup. The owner added chrome wheels and wide tires on the back, as well as a 1956 Ford car hood ornament to the hood. *Don Bunn collection*

The 1956 Custom cab "Big Back Window" option, popular with collectors today.

An F-100 Custom cab that is fitted with a long
bed, side-mounted spare and the popular "Big
Back Window" option. *Ford Motor Company*

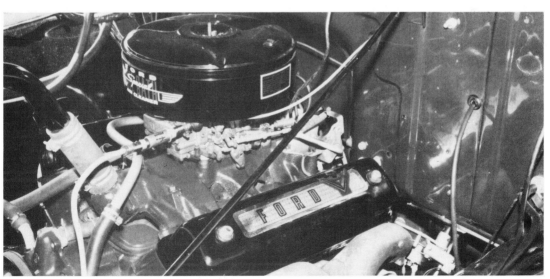

A 1956 Ford F-100 V-8 engine compartment. This particular truck is equipped with an optional dual-exhaust system. If it was equipped with the regular single exhaust system, a crossover pipe was run across the top of the engine.

The F-100 pickups have a timeless styling that still appeals to people today.

circle, something that was really appreciated in the tight confines of city work.

Another change to make Ford trucking a little easier in 1953 was the addition of a Ford-o-matic truck transmission for people who didn't like to shift gears or work a clutch. Though available only on the F-100s at first, this transmission option would be supplied for other light-duty trucks in later model years. On the regular manual transmission offerings, shifting of gears was made easier by adding synchronizers on second, third and fourth gears. For those wanting a little more economy a Warner Gear Overdrive transmission was added as an extracost option for F-100 vehicles just after the trucks were introduced.

For 1954 the big news at Ford concerned the release of a new overhead-valve-design V-8 engine to replace the old flathead that had been in use since 1932. This engine displaced the same 239 ci as before, but with its more modern design it was more efficient, stronger and built to last longer. This new design would also allow for increases in displacement in the future, whereas the old design had just about run its course, with no room for expansion. The six-cylinder engine was bored out to 223 ci and was nicknamed the Mileage Maker Six.

The rest of the changes for 1954, and for 1955 as well, involved mostly alterations to trim like grilles, nameplates and so on.

It was a different story in 1956, though, as Ford revamped the upper cab areas and doors to accept a new, full, wraparound windshield. A new popular option also involved changing the back glass area to form what Ford called its Big Window option. This option added quite a bit of glass area and is much sought after today by 1956 Ford truck aficionados. Though they were stopgap measures meant to update the looks of this Ford design for one more year, these two

A 1956 Ford F-100 pickup bed could haul quite a load, as this factory promotional photo shows. *Don Bunn collection*

changes have helped make 1956 the most popular year for collectible Ford trucks.

Another change made on the 1956 Ford trucks was the switch to a 12 volt electrical system, replacing the 6 volt systems used before. Still another change involved a redesigned grille bar that was available in white paint or in a chrome-plated finish. The chrome-plated grille was standard with the Custom Cab Package or optional at extra cost for Standard models. This was the first time since the thirties that a chromed grille appeared on a Ford truck.

Ford also added one more model to the 1956 F-100 range of vehicles to give them more market coverage. This model came with a long pickup box rather than a short box like that found on regular pickups. This longer box was like the express boxes found

From the doors forward this 1956 Australian Ford Ute looks like a regular 1956 US Ford Mainline, but from the doors back it is all Australian. *Gary Hallett*

A rare 1956 Courier sedan delivery. This one has been dressed up a bit with Fairlane trim, factory fender skirts, factory spotlights and a factory grille guard. Most Courier models in 1956 were a lot plainer.

This Courier is a 1955 model that has had some Fairlane trim applied to brighten up the exterior. Note the special, one-piece side-opening cargo door used on the Courier models.

The two-tone paint scheme on this 1956 F-100 Custom cab adds a nice touch. This truck is also equipped with the "Big Back Window" option, radio and a tarp cover.

on the F-250 and F-350 trucks and required the F-100 so equipped to use a longer-wheelbase chassis.

When all was said and done, when the last 1956 Ford truck rolled off the assembly lines, some people wondered whether these trucks had worked out as well as the Bonus Built Fords that preceded them. The answer was that they sure had. For during this period Ford trucks increased their market share and did so in a shorter span of time—four years versus five. And these later models outsold their counterparts by more than 200,000 units. This figure was nothing to scoff at back in the early fifties when truck sales were nowhere near where they were in the early nineties when Ford sold more than 500,000 F Series trucks in a mediocre year.

The 1956 Ford F-100 hood side trim.

A 1956 F–350 Standard cab tow truck with a
two-tone dealer promotional paint job.

Chapter 8

1957–1960 Styleside and Flareside Trucks

★★★★★ 1957–1960 F–100 Styleside pickup
★★★★ 1957–1960 F–100 Flareside pickup
★★★ 1957–1960 F–100 panel
★★★ 1957–1960 Courier sedan delivery
★★★ 1957–1960 F–250 Styleside pickup
★★★ 1957–1960 F–350 pickup
★★★★ 1957 Ranchero
★★★★★ 1957 Custom Ranchero
★★★ 1957–1958 Marmon-Herrington all-wheel-drive
★★★ 1959–1960 Ford 4x4 pickup
★★★ 1957–1960 F Series stake/platform
★★ 1958–1960 F–250 Flareside pickup
★★ 1958–1960 F–350 Flareside pickup
★★★★ 1958–1959 Ranchero
★★★★ 1960 Falcon Ranchero

A little over a year after the 1953 Ford truck line was introduced, Ford's designers and engineers went back to the drawing boards to come up with a worthy successor to these trucks. Marketing surveys taken at that time were telling them that the American public was getting more style conscious. It wanted its vehicles, both car and truck, to reflect that feeling of modishness. Fashion and a bit of flamboyance had overtaken utility and function as primary concerns when thoughts turned to purchasing a new vehicle. This change in attitudes wasn't all that bad, as evidenced by some of the memorable cars and trucks that were products of this era.

Two noteworthy vehicles that fell into this category were the 1957 Ford cars and 1957 Ford trucks. Some of the best-looking Fords released during the fifties appeared in 1957. What makes these models stand out so much is their styling, which was a marked contrast to what came before. One version was not mistaken for the other.

In the case of the trucks, gone were the rounded curves and the fat fenders, replaced by sharp, clearly defined straight edges and just a suggestion of a fender. These trucks were definitely from the slab-sided school of design. They featured a look that was modern and more stylish than that of any Ford that preceded them. Their styling was the big news for 1957.

1957–1960 Production

Year	Model Courier	Ranchero	F–100	F–250	F–350	P-100, P-350 and P–400	Total
1957	6,172	21,695	113,622	19,624	14,219	3,770	179,102
1958	3,352	9,950	104,581	17,404	13,324	3,287	151,898
1959	5,141	14,169	157,063	26,761	21,092	5,062	229,288
1960	2,374	21,027	174,037	30,991	21,363	5,746	255,538
Grand total							815,826

A full-color, two-page ad that appeared in the March 1957 issue of the *Farm Journal*. Jerry Bougher

In 1957 a Colorado Coroner traveled in style at the wheel of this 1957 Ford Courier sedan delivery, which had been converted for this particular use. This Courier looks as if it has been fitted with a regular station wagon two-piece tailgate instead of the one-piece cargo door that was originally fitted.

Also making news this year in the Ford truck camp was a chic pickup called the Ranchero. This pickup variant was based on the two-door Ranch Wagon station wagon body, as was the redesigned 1957 Courier. The Ranchero featured the same sensational styling found on the 1957 Ford passenger-car line upon which it was based. It was a true dual-purpose vehicle in that it could be used as a truck or a car depending on the situation. Ford promoted it by saying it could do a day's work and could then be driven to the country club for dinner. Ford offered two models of the Ranchero: the base model simply called the Ranchero or the more upscale version called the Custom Ranchero series. The Custom Ranchero offered quite a few extras, making for quite a stylish vehicle.

Taking a cue from Chevrolet in its regular pickup line Ford offered two types of pickup

For 1958 the Ranchero models used the 1958 style front-end treatment, but from the doors back everything except the trim was carried over from 1957. This two-tone model is a Custom Ranchero. *Ford Motor Company*

In 1959 there was only one Ranchero model offered, the Custom Ranchero. This one has been personalized with factory accessories like optional mirrors, fender ornaments and fender skirts.

models. Type one was called the Flareside, and it offered a narrow bed flanked by two wide rear fenders. Type number two was called the Styleside, and it received a wide pickup box where the fenders were located inside its slab sides. Chevrolet started this slab-sided trend in 1955 with its Cameo pickup, but Ford outdid it by offering the choice of either type at no additional cost. The Cameo was priced much higher than a regular Chevrolet pickup because its body sides were made of fiberglass bonded to the sides of a regular steel pickup box; that extra work required extra costs, and those costs were passed on to the buyer. The Ford boxes didn't require any additional work, so Ford didn't have to charge anything extra for them. This slab-sided look really caught on with the public, as the Styleside became the most popular body style of the 1957 model year. The new Styleside treatment could even be called a trendsetter, considering how many similar pickup bodies were released after it.

As to styling changes, the new Ford cabs and associated front-end pieces were all-new for 1957. The cab was wider, lower and a little bit longer than the cabs that were fitted to the 1953–1956 trucks. It also featured more glass area, making it a little brighter than before. The new models had wider, flatter hoods, whose sides were designed to match up to the fender edges, producing a straight line from the top of the hood to the lower side of the fender. These fenders weren't fenders at all in the old sense because they were just flat-sided pieces of sheet metal that covered the wheelhouse area. To break up a straight look and add some excitement in this area some character lines were pressed into the metal to suggest the arc of a fender. To break up the body from front to back a character line

Prior to 1959, if a customer needed a 4x4 truck his new Ford was taken to an outside contractor for such a modification. In 1959, Ford jumped on the 4x4 bandwagon by releasing its own light-duty 4x4. This factory photograph shows just such a model with a chrome grille. *Ford Motor Company*

A 1960 Ford F–100 Custom cab Styleside pick-up, finished in a Monte Carlo Red and White paint scheme. Under the hood is the original 223 ci Mileage Maker Six that Ford installed thirty years ago. *Deb Schissler*

was started just behind the headlights and went through the door area and all the way to the back on Styleside models. This character line made a good separation line on trucks that featured two-tone paint jobs.

The model line-up was the same in 1957 as in previous years, and the driveline components were also carried over.

For 1958 everything stayed mostly the same for the F Series Ford trucks. They received a new grille and dual headlights, and halfway through the model year the 292 ci Y-block V-8 replaced the 272 ci as the optional engine to the 223 ci Mileage Maker Six, which was the base powerplant.

The Ranchero and Courier models featured the new 1958 Ford passenger car styling except on the back end where both vehicles retained the look of the 1957 models. They were available with a wider range of powerplants, including the 223 ci six, the Y-block V-8s and the newly released FE fam-ily in 332 ci or 352 ci displacement.

For 1959 the F Series of trucks remained relatively the same except for a change in hood and grille designs. The hood now had a large vent area that housed Ford letters. That was about it for styling changes. However, some big news came in the 1959 Ford light-duty truck line, and it revolved around the first factory four-wheel-drive units to ever appear in a Ford catalog.

Before 1959 if one wanted a Ford four-wheel-drive vehicle one had to go to an aftermarket supplier or modifier to have such a conversion done. The most famous Ford four-wheel-drives for more than twenty years were the Marmon-Herrington All Wheel Drive trucks. Marmon-Herrington offered converted Ford vehicles in four-wheel-drive, and in some cases six-wheel-drive was offered. Before 1959 Ford wanted no part of this business, but in that year it decided that it wanted some of the action, so it chose to get involved. You could still get a Marmon-Herrington-converted light-duty Ford truck in 1959, but these trucks were exceptions rather than the rule. Marmon-Herrington was still converting Fords to All Wheel Drive form in the early nineties, but most of its Ford work was done on medium- and heavy-duty units.

For 1959 the Ranchero and Courier sedan deliveries featured the all-new body designs from the passenger-car line. The Ranchero was available in one model only, the Custom Ranchero. The Courier, which before had steel sideboard panels covering the rear side windows, now featured glass all the way around the body. It was now referred to as the commercial ranch wagon or the Courier. Also changed on these new Couriers was the tailgate, which was now the regular station wagon two-piece affair rather than the special single-door arrangement.

No big changes were made in the F Series of Ford trucks for 1960; the only differences seen were in the grille and hood treatment.

This was the last year for this body style and for an F Series panel delivery truck in the United States. It was also the last year for a full-size sedan delivery vehicle for Ford. Hereafter any vehicle of this nature for Ford would be found on a smaller platform.

The big news in the 1960 model year for Ford light-duty commercial vehicles involved the Ranchero, which was now a model found on the compact Falcon platform. The new Ranchero was much smaller than the old Ranchero and about 1,000 lb. lighter, but its payload rating almost matched the previous version's. With a 144 ci six-cylinder powerplant, it was also much more economical than the old Ranchero, a fact that Ford promoted in all Ranchero advertising this year.

Though the redesigned stylish Ford trucks of this period have a lot going for them, collectors today prefer the 1953–1956 models. In either case, no matter which ones you prefer, they both make for some nice collectibles.

1961–1966 New Look Trucks

For the 1961 model year the big news at Ford concerned its redesigned F Series of trucks and a new line of economy vehicles it called, appropriately, the Econoline.

This new line of commercial vehicles comprised three models: the Econoline pickup, Econoline delivery van and Econoline station bus. The delivery van was a direct replacement for the F-100 panel delivery, which was no longer made in the United States. The delivery van proved to be the most popular of the three, with sales of more than 32,000 units in its first year. Sales of the pickup and the station bus were about equal,

The Falcon Sedan Delivery made its debut in 1961 to join the Falcon Ranchero as Ford's Commercial Economy Twins. *Ford Motor Company*

When painted in a two-tone fashion, as seen on this 1961 Falcon Ranchero, the Ranchero took on a more deluxe, upscale look. The wide whitewalls add to the look, too. *Ford Motor Company*

This factory promotional photo shows an Econoline pickup that has been fitted with a "Big Back Window" option. It also has a radio, as noted by the cowl-mounted antenna sitting on the right side. *Ford Motor Company*

A 1962 Falcon Ranchero. The similar 1961 model used a different grille design. *Ford Motor Company*

with each being about half that of the van. After 1961 the station bus was marketed under the Falcon name. All three models were of a unibody construction and were powered by the same six-cylinder engine that was used in the Falcon. They also shared other common parts with the Falcon to try to keep manufacturing costs down.

The Ranchero was still a Falcon in 1961 and was joined by another Falcon commer-

cial car. This one was called the Falcon sedan delivery, and like the Ranchero it was based on a two-door Falcon station-wagon platform. The sedan delivery was meant to appeal to the same customers who bought Couriers before. Both the Ranchero and the Falcon sedan delivery used the same body style as the 1960 Falcons, with the only exterior change being a new grille to help differentiate between the two.

F Series fans saw a restyled truck line that featured some softening up of the body lines as well as some resculpturing in lines and accents. Gone was the sharp, squared-off slab-sided look prevalent on the 1957–1960 models. That look was replaced by the rounding off of some corners and the additional use of side sculpturing on the cab, hood and body sides. These trucks featured new cabs, interiors, hoods, bumpers, grilles and bodies too.

Once again pickup buyers were offered their choice of either a Flareside box or the more stylish Styleside, in either short- or long-box form. The Styleside version featured a unique integral cab-and-body arrangement rather than a separate cab and body, as is usually the case. The cab and body

In 1962 Ford offered a wide range of commercial vehicles to suit different needs. This is an F-100 Styleside at a construction site. *Ford Motor Company*

The interior of a Deluxe Falcon station bus. Note the plush door panels, deluxe dash layout and the floor-mounted heater. *Ford Motor Company*

joined together offered a carlike uninterrupted line from front to back. It was a stylish concept to say the least, but Ford found a little buyer resistance to this new look, so in later years it offered an additional Styleside model that used a separate bed, as normal pickups do. Rather than design a new bed for this added model, Ford just retained the same bed that it had used in the 1957–1960 Styleside line. This bed was featured through 1962 and 1963 for the F-100 and F-250 until a restyled separate bed appeared for these trucks in 1964. The F-350 models using a separate bed retained the 1957–1960 style through 1966.

Ford also found one other problem with the integral cab-and-body concept, and that had to do with its four-wheel-drive pickups. Ford feared that with all the twisting a 4x4 chassis went through, this type of body would be damaged, so it offered the 4x4 option only on the Flareside models in the early part of 1961 production. A few Styleside 4x4s were built toward the end of the model year, but these units were equipped with the earlier-style separate pickup box.

Things stayed pretty much the same for 1962 and 1963 in the light-duty truck ranks

The 1962 F-100 Flareside long-bed pickups were never produced in great numbers.

103

A line-up that couldn't be beat in 1964. This shot, taken at the Ford Proving Grounds, shows an F Series pickup, Ranchero, and Econoline pickup and van. There's also a camper and a stake model too. *Ford Motor Company*

Two-tone paint jobs like the one on this 1964 F-100 Styleside pickup really add excitement to the looks of the trucks.

at Ford, except for some minor trim changes as well as some changes in engine and transmission choices. Chief among these alterations was the addition of a V–8 engine to the Ranchero and sedan delivery Falcons in 1963. With this step the Falcon-based vehicles were starting to move away from their economy roots.

Some styling changes were afoot for the 1964 model year in the F Series line as well as for the compact Falcon Ranchero and sedan delivery. The Ranchero and sedan delivery were restyled so that they looked completely different than the Rancheros and sedan deliveries of before. They were stylish rather than being plain looking, as they were

A beautiful two-tone 1965 F-100 Flareside.
Steven Williams

The 1965 Custom cab F Series interior. Note the
two-tone treatment on the dash panel, door
panels and seat upholstery.

The restyled pickup box, which made its debut on the 1964 series. Before this box came out, if one wanted a separate pickup box they had to accept a 1957–1960 style unit.

The 1965 F Series engine compartment. This is a 352 ci V–8, an engine that became available in light-duty Ford trucks at the time.

In 1966 the only Styleside pickup box available for the F-350 trucks was the old 1957-1960 style. This Custom cab version of a 1966 F-350 is a factory 4x4 unit.

The engine compartment showing a Y-Block V-8 of 292 ci. Note the crossover exhaust pipe, linkage details and the FoMoCo script on the voltage regulator. *Ford Motor Company*

If you like the looks of the Econoline but need a pickup truck, you might consider an Econoline pickup.

This factory promotional postcard released in 1966 shows two Econoline vans. The regular model and the new Super extended version.

Pre-production 1966 F Series cab layout details. Note the four-speed transmission lever and four-wheel-drive selector. Also note the only instrument shown is the speedometer. *Ford Motor Company*

before. They were still economy vehicles, especially when powered by six-cylinder engines, but they sure didn't look the part anymore.

Over on the F Series side of the house the integral cab-and-body Styleside pickups were gone, as was the old-style fifties box. The F-100 and F-250 featured a new pickup box design that looked more natural in this context. When ordered with a Styleside box the F-350 unfortunately still retained the old-style box because Ford didn't think its lower production numbers warranted a separate restyled box. In any event, for those who didn't like the straight-sided look Ford still offered the choice of a Flareside model in all three series.

Though the 1965 Ford F Series trucks looked similar to the 1964 models they replaced, quite a bit of change was going on under the skin on these trucks. The biggest change was the replacement of the mono-beam front axle on the F-100 and F-250 with a new independent front suspension system. Ford called this new suspension a Twin I-Beam system, and that is basically what it was: a front axle that consisted of two separate beams that were coil spring suspended and joined in the center by a support mechanism that allowed both axles to move up and down independently of each other. Such a system gave a much better ride than the old straight-bar arrangement used before on

these Fords. Ford promoted this new concept heavily during the model year in all of its truck advertising.

A restyled Ranchero and a new utility vehicle led the parade of Ford truck changes for the 1966 model year. The Ranchero used the same styling as the Falcon station wagons of this year, and it was the only commercial vehicle found in the line. Ford dropped the sedan delivery because there was no longer sufficient demand for this type vehicle. The year 1966 was the last for the Falcon Ranchero also, because starting in 1967 it would be moved up and onto the Fairlane platform.

The new series of utility vehicles that Ford released in 1966 was called the Bronco. This line consisted of three models: a pickup, a roadster and a station wagon. The roadster was the base model, and it was designed to operate with only the barest of necessities. By bare I mean a body, a seat and a fully operational chassis. These models in base form came without doors or a top. This model was meant to go up against the Jeep and the International Scout, which were also

The 1966 Falcon Ranchero was a handsome vehicle, one of the best-looking Rancheros to carry the Falcon label. It's too bad that this body styling was used for only one model year.

offered in a base, no-frills mode. Though these Broncos and the other models like them were bare in base form, Ford made sure enough extra-cost optional equipment was available to cater to just about any 4x4 off-roaders taste. These models came with a six-cylinder engine and a three-speed manual transmission in base form, on a four-wheel-drive chassis. The pickup model came with a short top and doors, and the station wagon came with doors and a top that covered the passenger compartment. To prove that these vehicles were as tough as the competition Ford hired Bill Stroppe to prepare some Broncos for off-road racing, and these Broncos did quite well against the likes of modified Jeeps and Scouts.

The rest of the news concerning other vehicles in the light-duty commercial class of 1966 was limited to minor updates like grille and trim changes.

A Highway Cruiser Camper unit was featured on this F-250 Camper Special Pickup in 1965. This truck is equipped with a 352 ci V-8 engine, heavy-duty truck tires, clearance lights, western mirrors and deluxe side trim moldings. *Ford Motor Company*

This restored 1966 F-100 Custom cab has features that have been borrowed from a later-model Explorer. Those mag-style wheel covers and bumper guards were offered on the 1970 Explorer.

A 1966 F-350 Styleside truck. *Ford Motor Company*

Chapter 10

1967–1977 Modern Trucks

★★★★★	1967–1977 Ranchero
★★★★	1967–1977 Bronco
★★★★	1967–1977 F-100 Styleside pickup
★★★	1967–1977 F-250/F-350 Styleside pickup
★★★	1967–1977 F-100, F-250, F-350 Flareside pickup
★★★★	1967–1977 F Series 4x4 pickup
★★★	1967–1977 F Series platform/stake
★★★	1967–1977 Econoline van
★★★	1967–1977 Club Wagon
★★★	1972–1977 Courier pickup
★★★	1976–1977 Cruisin' van

For 1967 Ford's F Series trucks and the Ranchero featured new designs, whereas the Bronco and Econoline featured the same styling as before.

The F Series line went back to a squared-off slab-sided look. Cab, fenders, pickup boxes, hoods, grilles, bumpers and trim were all new designs. Breaking up the body and cab sides was an extruded spear molding that ran from front to back. The rocker panels were tucked in at the bottom, helping to break up a too flat look.

The F Series cabs were revised with more glass area, more shoulder room and a wider seat. Other interior features that were new included a color-keyed padded dash, a foot-operated parking brake, an emergency flasher switch, two-speed wipers, seatbelts for driver and right-side passenger, a one-piece hardboard headliner, bright aluminum scuff plates, a redesigned instrument cluster and color-keyed vinyl seat covers in red, blue, green or beige. Safetywise, all Ford trucks and cars this year featured dual-reservoir master brake cylinders.

This time around and until it went out of production the Ranchero was based on an intermediate-size Fairlane platform. Buyers had their choice of three models. The Fairlane Ranchero was the base model, the Fairlane 500 Ranchero the middle and the Fairlane 500 XL Ranchero the top of the line. The Fairlane 500 Ranchero was a deluxe offering that came with such nice features as cut pile carpeting, electric clock, brightmetal trim panels, brightmetal wheelwell moldings, brightmetal full wheel covers and bodyside pinstriping. Color-keyed interiors of red, blue, parchment or Ivy Gold were offered. The Fairlane 500 XL Ranchero was an even more deluxe version, having all the equipment found in the 500 model plus a console, bucket seats, deluxe rocker panel trim and 500 XL badges.

Powertrain choices ranged from a 200 ci six to a 390 ci 320 hp GT engine that gave the Ranchero some pretty spirited performance.

The Bronco for 1967 looked the same as before, but a few changes surfaced on this model, like self-adjusting brakes, a dual-braking-system master cylinder, back-up lights and variable-rate wipers. For the

The 1967 F Series Flareside long-bed models are hard to find today because there weren't many of them originally built.

111

Econoline the only real change was the switch to a dual-reservoir master cylinder.

1967 F Series Options
Dual rear wheels (F–350)
Deluxe two-tone paint (F–100, F–250
   Stylesides)
Engines
   300 ci 170 hp 6 cylinder
   352 ci 208 hp V–8
Transmissions
   4 speed manual
   Cruise-O-Matic
   Overdrive (F–100)
Heavy-duty black vinyl seat trim
Deluxe fresh air heater
AM radio
Dual electric horns
Air conditioning
Supplemental 25 gallon fuel tank
Limited-slip differential
Larger tires
Power steering
Mirrors
Full wheel covers
Camper bodies
Camper caps
Two-tone paint
Camper Special Package: 70 amp-hr
   battery, oil pressure and ammeter
   gauges, Deluxe fresh air heater, dual
   electric horns, chrome Western mirrors,
   extra cooling radiator, Camper Special
   nameplates, camper wiring harness,
   relocated tailpipe, heavy-duty shocks
Custom Cab Package: Color-coordinated
   woven plastic seat trim in red, blue,
   green or beige; armrests on both doors;
   rubber floor mat; cigar lighter; bright-
   trimmed horn ring; instrument cluster;
   grille and headlight trim; windshield;
   headliner retainer molding; padded dash;
   Custom Cab nameplates
Ranger Package: Color-keyed armrests,
   nylon carpeting, vinyl seat coverings
   with a soft cloth appearance, vinyl door
   trim panels, bright-finished horn ring,
   instrument cluster, front bumper, grille,
   wheel covers, wheel lip moldings, rocker
   panel moldings, dashboard, headliner
   moldings

The second-generation Econoline bore no external resemblance to the model it replaced. *Ford Motor Company*

1968–1972
The year 1968 was the year of the Ranchero and the Econoline because both series were extensively changed. For the second consecutive year the Rancheros featured a total restyling job. Their new body reflected the changes seen in the new Torino and Fairlane models. It was now a little longer, a little wider and a little heavier. It was also more sculptured, in marked contrast to the straight-sided design the Ranchero employed in 1966 and 1967. Windshields, roofs and glass were changed, as well as the seat, headliner and dash-panel setup.

The Ranchero was still available in three series, but one change in nomenclature occurred. The top-of-the-line Ranchero was no longer the 500 XL; the new ruler of the hill was the Ranchero GT. This GT included the same trick equipment found on the 500 XL model of the year before plus a set of special GT wheels, GT badges and a set of reflective side C-stripes that were similar to the ones on the Ford GT race cars that won at Le Mans. Engines for the Ranchero once again started with the 200 ci six and went all the way to the top with a 428 ci Cobra Jet—a combination that could really light your fire.

As far as the Econoline goes, Ford originally planned to introduce a redesigned version of its popular vans in the fall of 1967 with its other 1968 truck models. But a long strike between the United Automobile Workers and Ford put that plan on the back burner. Even after the strike ended, it took

Two of Ford's special truck models released for the 1969 model year. The top photo shows a Farm & Ranch Special, while the photo below shows a Ranger. *Ford Motor Company*

Ford awhile to get back up to production levels that were the same as before, so the introduction of a new model had to wait a little bit longer. Thus the new Econolines weren't released until the model year was half over. Ordinarily a model release this late might be referred to as a 1968½, for example. But Ford called these new models 1969s. Ford did produce and sell some Econolines before the release of the 1969 models, but those were carryover 1967 models.

Whether you call them 1968½s or 1969s these new Econolines looked quite different from the first series built from 1961 through 1967. They were longer, wider and heavier. Restyled from stem to stern, they looked like no other vans on the market back then. With their short hoods, larger grilles and repositioned front axles they set a styling statement that the others would follow.

The new Econolines were available in three series, the E-100, the E-200 and the E-300. In each series three models were offered, a cargo van, a window van and a display van. The cargo van was a regular van without any windows in the cargo area, the display van featured windows on the right

side of the body and the window van had windows on both sides. For customers who wanted a van that was a passenger vehicle Ford offered its club wagon, custom club wagon, and Chateau club wagon. As you may imagine by its title, the last version was the top-of-the-line model.

On the bottom side the Econolines now featured a Twin I-Beam front axle and

The 1969 F-250 Crew Cabs like this one were sometimes seen around construction sites back then. This battered example has been around quite a few job sites over the years.

For 1969, Ford changed the Bronco with a grille facelift and some new engine options. The same changes made their way to the Ranchero. *Ford Motor Company*

1968 Bronco Options

Bucket seats
Cigarette lighter
Cab doors (roadster)
Closed crankcase emission system
Heavy-duty clutch
Tailgate mount for spare tire
Heavy-duty battery
Rear bench seat
Front bumper guards
Heavy-duty alternator
Limited-slip front axle
Limited-slip rear axle
Extra Cooling Package
Chrome bumpers
Grille guard
Armrests
Bumper guards
Wheel covers
Tailgate moldings
Canvas top (roadster)
289 ci V–8 engine
Bodyside moldings
Heavy Duty GVW Package
Auxiliary fuel tank
Tonneau cover
Tow hooks
Sport Package (wagons and pickups): Dual armrests, wheel covers, vinyl mat on floor in station wagon, cigarette lighter, hardboard headliner, chrome windshield molding, chrome side window frames and instrument panel trim, chrome-plated bumpers and bumper guards

longer rear leaf springs, both changes improving the ride quality of these vehicles. Engine choices included two six-cylinders, at 170 ci and 240 ci, and Ford's 302 ci V–8.

The rest of the changes seen on other Ford light-duty vehicles in 1968 amounted to some grille updates, trim changes and the installation of side marker lights on most models.

No changes of note were made on the 1969 Ford commercial light-duty vehicles.

Most alterations, except for the Bronco, involved redesigned grilles and other trim updates. In the Bronco line the roadster model was dropped and the station wagon top was no longer removable. The windshield was now of a fixed-in-place design, so it could no longer be folded flat.

When the 1970 model year rolled around no changes were on tap for the Econoline, Broncos or F Series trucks. However, the Ranchero featured an all-new design.

1969 Engine Line-up

Displacement	Horsepower	Type	Application
170 ci	105 hp	6 cylinder	Bronco, Econoline
240 ci	150 hp	6 cylinder	Econoline, F Series
250 ci	155 hp	6 cylinder	Ranchero
289 ci	195 hp	V–8	Bronco
300 ci	165 hp	6 cylinder	F Series
302 ci	220 hp	V–8	Econoline, F Series, Ranchero
351 ci	250 hp	V–8	Ranchero
351 ci	290 hp	V–8	Ranchero
360 ci	215 hp	V–8	F Series
390 ci	255 hp	V–8	F Series
390 ci	320 hp	V–8	Ranchero
428 ci	335 hp	V–8	Ranchero
428 ci	335 hp	V–8 Cobra Jet Ram Air	Ranchero

Specialized user packages like this Turtle Top camper conversion showed how versatile Ford's 1969 Club Wagons were. *Ford Motor Company*

Although it looks similar to a Falcon Ranchero built in the United States, there are enough differences between the Australian Falcon Utility and its US counterpart to easily tell the two apart. The model shown here is a 1968 XT Falcon Utility. *Ford Motor Company Ltd, Australia*

Two Ford 1969 specials. The one shown above is the Contractor's Special (note the toolboxes), while the bottom photo shows a Camper Special. *Ford Motor Company*

The restyled body that was seen on the Ranchero was sleeker than before. It was also more stylish and quite a bit more aerodynamically clean. The front end now came to a point rather than being blunt-nosed. A new model was also added to the Ranchero line to help it appeal to a wider audience. This was called the Ranchero Squire pickup, and like the station wagon model it had Country Squire type paneling on its body sides. In this guise you probably wouldn't have any trouble parking it at the country club. With this much luxury this model became the top banana in the Ranchero line, replacing the GT. The GT was still the sporty model, with the Ranchero being the base model again and the Ranchero 500 being a little more deluxe in execution.

Though no big changes were planned for the F Series trucks, Ford marketing went off in a different direction this year to widen their market appeal. It did this by offering a number of special models meant to appeal to different market segments and needs. For instance the base F Series pickup was now called the Custom pickup, and if a buyer was looking for something a little out of the ordinary she or he could order a new F Series truck with one of the following special packages: Sport Custom Cab, Ranger, Camper Special, Farm and Ranch Special, Contractor Special, Heavy Duty Special, Ranger XLT and Explorer Special.

This shotgun approach to marketing produced the desired results, as Ford increased its market share to 36.5 percent of the truck business in the United States in 1970.

Once again changes for the 1971 line of Ford light-duty trucks involved grille and trim updates. For the F Series Ford stayed with its "specials" marketing program and even expanded that program to cover three more models. Now buyers had nine different F Series specials from which to choose. This program worked out so well that Ford

This 1969 Club Wagon looks sharp with its bright grille, bumpers and hubcaps. This one also has a body-side protection molding to help ward off nicks and parking lot dents. *Ford Motor Company*

The year is 1970 and we see two of Ford's special truck models for that particular model year. The top photo is the Ranger, while the bottom photo is the Ranger XLT. The former was a deluxe model while the latter was sort of a super deluxe variant. *Ford Motor Company*

FORD's COURIER... WINS BAJA 500

When we think of Courier pickups we usually think of economy trucks. But as this Ford promotional postcard shows some of them were also racing champions.

even offered some specials to Econoline, Bronco and Ranchero buyers too.

Ford entered the minipickup class in 1972 with a badge-engineered Mazda model it called the Courier. By going this route, Ford had a model to compete with the likes of similar models from Datsun and Toyota. It took this action to give itself some time to develop a model of its own. However, this arrangement worked out so well for both Ford and Mazda that Ford didn't feel the need to rush its version into production. As a matter of fact, its Ranger wasn't released until 1982.

The Courier wasn't the only Ford pickup to make news this year. Also making a bow was a restyled Ranchero that was bigger, bolder and more muscular looking than the Rancheros of before. This new body featured a wide-mouth protruding grille on the front and a Coke-bottle-shaped body that curved out in its center section and tucked back in at its rocker panels. A sense of excitement flowed from the front of the body to the back, especially on the GT mod-

els with their wide, reflective laser side striping treatment.

This restyled Ranchero now sat on a full separate frame, something that hadn't been

---

1971 Ranger XLT Package

Styleside pickups and chassis-and-cab models
Mag-style full wheel covers
Wood-grain appliqué on tailgate
Whitewall tires
Bumper hitch
Rear-of-cab cargo light
Woodtone appliqués on door panels
Brightmetal wheelwell lips
Chrome-plated bumpers
Pleated cloth-and-vinyl seat covers
Color-keyed carpet
Brightmetal bodyside moldings
Perforated headliner
More insulation
Convenience Group
Color-keyed pleated vinyl door panels

A 1972 F-100 Styleside with the Ranger XLT
Package. *Ford Motor Company*

1972 Ranchero Options

SelectAire Conditioner
Power steering
AM/FM stereo radio
AM radio
Deluxe wheel covers
Tinted glass
Ivy Glow or Gold Glow special paint
Trailer Towing Packages (Class II, Class III)
Rim Blow Sport steering wheel
Electric clock
Sport-type racing mirrors
Black painted hood
Power front disc brakes
Vinyl roof (white or black)
High-back bucket seats
15 in. wheels
Performance tires
Mag wheels
V-8 engines (351 ci, 302 ci, 429 ci)
4 speed transmission with Hurst shifter

Selectshift transmission
Protection Group: Chrome bumper
guards, Flight bench seat, door edge
guards, vinyl insert bodyside molding,
cloth seat covers
Visibility Group: Lighted ashtray,
glovebox and parking brake indicator;
seatbelt light; underhood light
Performance Handling Package (351 ci and
429 ci engines): Heavy-duty springs,
shocks, large front stabilizer bar, rear
stabilizer bar
Ranchero Special Package: Ivy Glow or
Gold Glow paint, green or brown vinyl
roof, bright wheel lip moldings, front
bumper guards, Sport cloth interior with
color-coordinated vinyl trim (black for
Ivy Glow, ginger for Gold Glow), Sport
mirrors, brightmetal hubcaps with
brightmetal trim rings

By its car-type wheel covers, chrome-plated bumper guards, mirrors, box rails and side moldings, we can tell that this 1971 F Series Pickup is equipped with that year's Explorer Package. *Ford Motor Company*

seen on a Ranchero since the 1959 models. As if that wasn't enough change, Rancheros also came with redesigned interiors.

The Econoline Series also saw some changes for 1972, and chief among them was a new sliding side cargo door option in addition to the double-door version. This slid- ing-door arrangement made loading and un-loading easier, especially in tight, confined areas. Also new to the Econoline model line-up were special cutaway models consisting of a cutaway cab that could be joined with aftermarket bodies like chassis-mounted campers and vans. These cutaways featured fully dressed-out cabs with doors sitting atop a fully equipped chassis.

The F Series trucks got a new grille and some trim upgrades, and more special packages from which to choose. The Broncos got some revisions and more optional equipment to boot. And that basically covers all the changes that were seen through the 1972 model year.

1972 Engine Line-up

Displacement	Type	Application
110 ci	4 cylinder	Courier
170 ci	6 cylinder	Bronco, Econoline
250 ci	6 cylinder	Ranchero
302 ci	V-8	Bronco, Ranchero, F Series, Econoline
240 ci	6 cylinder	Econoline
300 ci	6 cylinder	F Series
360 ci	V-8	F Series
390 ci	V-8	F Series
351 ci	V-8	Ranchero
351 ci 4V	V-8	Ranchero
400 ci	V-8	Ranchero
429 ci	V-8	Ranchero

1973-1976

The year 1973 saw a few changes in Ford's light-duty model line-up. Starting with the Ranchero Ford designers redid the front grille and header panel, and added a 5 mph energy-absorbing bumper to the front end. This bumper design was nicknamed the Cow Catcher because it had a tacked-on look like that of the cowcatchers once on train locomotives. Other new features on the Ranchero were an inside hood release and improved rear brakes. The three models that

The brightmetal grille treatment dresses up the looks of this 1972 Econoline E-200 Cargo van. Such niceties made the vans look less like base-model commercial vehicles. *Ford Motor Company*

The 1973 Ford Ranger XLT pickups came with deluxe features like rocker panel moldings, body-side trim, car-type wheel covers, drip rail moldings and a windshield band. *Ford Motor Company*

constituted the Ranchero line were the base Ranchero 500, the midrange Ranchero GT and the top-of-the-line Ranchero Squire.

For Bronco buyers only one model was available and that was the station wagon. The Econoline vehicles stayed about the same, as did the Couriers.

The F Series trucks received some significant changes. They had larger, redesigned cabs and redesigned front fenders, hoods, bodies and frames. The larger cabs were also somewhat longer, which provided them with some open space behind the seat for in-cab storage. Engine choices included a 300 ci six and four V–8s ranging from 302 ci to 460 ci.

For 1974 things stayed pretty much the same with all of Ford's light-duty commercial vehicles, except for the addition of a new model in the F Series line. This new model, called a Super Cab, was an extended-cab version available in F–100, F–250 and F–350 forms. The Super Cabs came with Styleside pickup boxes in short, 6¾ ft. or long, 8 ft. length. Inside the extended part of the cab was a full-width, narrowed bench seat or two facing jump seats. The Super Cabs sat

on a stronger frame than was usually found under these trucks.

The year 1975 was the year of the Econoline because this series of trucks saw quite a few changes. Chief among the modifications seen on this third generation of Econolines was a redesigned front end that included a longer hood, longer front fenders and a new rectangular grille design. Other alterations involved door designs and the lengthening of the Econoline's wheelbase from 105 to 118 in. Most of that increase was achieved by relocating the front axle centerline to a more forward position.

Underneath the Econolines was now a full-length frame that added quite a bit of stiffness to the body. Before this change Econolines featured unitized construction rather than a body on a frame.

Some lesser changes were also noted on the Econolines this year. One involved shifting around some model designations and adding some new models to the line-up. For instance the E–100 Ford's base series Econoline was rated at half-ton and the E–200 series was rated at three-quarter-ton. But for the buyer who wanted something

A 1974 Ranger XLT F-250 in full deluxe trim.
Ford Motor Company

This 1974 two-tone Econoline E-300 Cargo Van looks almost too pretty to be parked at a construction site. Wonder how long those wheel covers and whitewalls stayed on it after this photo was taken. *Ford Motor Company*

1975 Engine Line-up

Displacement	Type	Application
110 ci	4 cylinder	Courier
200 ci	6 cylinder	Bronco
302 ci	V-8	Bronco, F-100
300 ci	6 cylinder	Econoline, F-100, F-250
351 ci	V-8	Econoline
460 ci	V-8	Econoline, F-250, F-350
351 ci	2V V-8	Ranchero
351 ci	4V V-8	Ranchero
400 ci	2V V-8	Ranchero
460 ci	4V V-8	Ranchero

Displacement	Type	Application
360 ci	V-8	F-250, F-350
390 ci	V-8	F-250, F-350

Free Wheelin' Package
Econoline
Black paint on bumpers, rocker panels and mirrors
Forged-aluminum wheels
Charcoal painted grille
Circular side windows
Spare tire cover
Full-length headlining
Wood-grain vinyl side panels (interior)
Full carpeting
Push bar (starting in May 1977)

A cutaway Econoline model that has been fitted with an aftermarket-sourced cube van body.
Ford Motor Company

Wild graphics and custom wheels help to set this 1975 Econoline Custom van apart from the crowd. There was plenty of room in the back to haul motorcycles and other gear to the country.

The Chateau Club Wagon was the top-of-the-line model for many years. This version features plaid upholstery and a two-tone paint finish. *Ford Motor Company*

The short, shallow engine compartment opening on the Econolines and Club Wagons allowed just enough space to check fluids in the battery and radiator, as well as the oil dipstick and the master cylinder. *Ford Motor Company*

in-between, like a heavy-duty half-ton, Ford added the E-150 series, which offered a little something extra. Between the E-200 and E-300, which was rated at one-ton, Ford added an extra series it called the E-250, which offered a heavy-duty three-quarter-ton vehicle to carry a little higher payload than the regular E-200 carried. And Ford didn't stop here either; for the camper and motor home manufacturers it offered a heavy-duty E-300 that it called the E-350. The E-350 was a perfect vehicle for such a conversion; the extra strength provided in its frame and suspension made hauling a portable dwelling around child's play.

In the F Series line Ford offered a new heavy-duty version of the F-100. This was called the F-150, and it fit a niche between the F-100 and the F-250. This series comprised about six vehicles, most of them being pickups.

The Bronco received a heavier-duty rear axle and front brakes for 1975. A new exhaust system was available, and a fuel

Ford Limited Edition Sale

Broncos, F Series pickups and Rancheros could all be had in 1976 with the Limited Edition

Explorer Package. Judging by all the 1976 Explorers I've seen it was a popular option.

filler neck redesign allowed the Bronco to be fueled only with unleaded gasoline. This filler neck was also used on the E–100 Econoline, the Courier, the Ranchero and some F–100 models.

With all the changes seen in the previous model year, alterations for 1976 were minor. Most involved trim and grille modifications. However, Ford did see fit to add to its light-duty line a couple of new models that catered to the new youth truck market, which was starting to gain some impressive numbers about this time. This new market wanted trucks that looked snazzy, and for it Ford brought back an old model that had been in mothballs for a while and introduced a new model that featured bright colorful graphics.

The old model brought back for the youth market was Ford's famous Shorty, a short, narrow pickup box that Ford offered on its Flareside series. This short box had been in use as far back as 1953, before it was

dropped in the early seventies. Regular pickup buyers preferred the extra room that was available with a Styleside body, which is why the Shorty body was dropped. But the kids liked the looks of the Shorty truck, and Ford sold quite a few examples of it under its

Have you ever wondered what an F Series Suburban might look like? This is the El Detalle, a model made in Mexico for that market.

If you wanted a customized factory pickup in the late 1970s, Ford's Free Wheelin' package was a neat way to go with white-spoke wheels, body-side striping, black-painted bumpers and a roll bar.

Have you ever heard of the Coors Courier before? Neither had I until I found this old Ford Motorsport postcard. The truck was never produced.

The 1979 Free Wheelin' Package on the "Shorty" F-100 Flareside included white-spoke wheels, white-letter tires, black grille and pinstriping. *Ford Motor Company*

A 1979 Ranchero GT in bright red with gold accents, the last model of a special breed. Note the sport mirrors, white-letter tires and slick GT striping. Add that all together and you have the Ranchero GT Package. *Ford Motor Company*

This 1979 F-350 Styleside pickup features the deluxe XLT Package that included extra trim pieces. *Ford Motor Company*

This 1979 Bronco Ranger XLT model has been outfitted with Ford's Free Wheelin' graphics package. The tri-color decals really added a racy flavor. *Ford Motor Company*

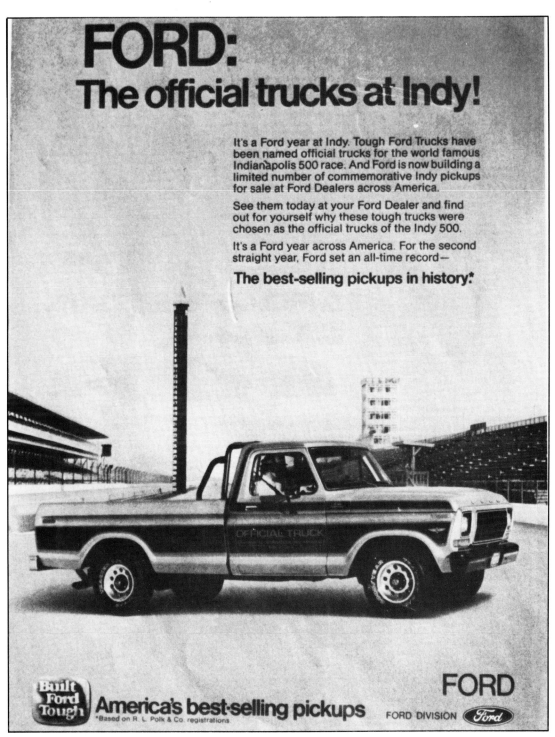

FORD:
The official trucks at Indy!

It's a Ford year at Indy. Tough Ford Trucks have been named official trucks for the world famous Indianapolis 500 race. And Ford is now building a limited number of commemorative Indy pickups for sale at Ford Dealers across America.

See them today at your Ford Dealer and find out for yourself why these tough trucks were chosen as the official trucks of the Indy 500.

It's a Ford year across America. For the second straight year, Ford set an all-time record—

The best-selling pickups in history.*

OFFICIAL TRUCK

Built Ford Tough America's best-selling pickups
*Based on R. L. Polk & Co. registrations

FORD

FORD DIVISION *Ford*

Although Ford-powered cars had appeared at the Indy 500 race on numerous occasions, the only time a Ford truck played a supporting role was in 1979. In honor of this occasion Ford ran some special Indy 500 Truck ads in the magazines.

Off-road racers like Ford products because they are tough trucks. This 1978 F-100 "Shorty" Flareside has an aluminum bed, full racing roll-cage and a race-prepped engine under the hood.

Ford called this highly modified Econoline their Hot Air Balloon Van. It made the show circuit rounds in the late 1970s, and featured hydraulically operated ramp doors to lift the balloon and basket into the cargo area, as well as a complete weather monitoring system.

Free Wheeling promotions over the next couple of years.

The new model introduced for the youth market was an Econoline cruising van that featured special silver paint with black, orange and magenta striping. On the inside it featured captain's chairs and other goodies meant to appeal to a "vanner." For the first time in vanning history a buyer could purchase a modified van right from the manufacturer. This model and the Shorty pickup helped Ford to get a toehold in the youth market segment, which would grow in importance in the years to come.

1977

After five model years of wearing the same skin, the Ranchero models were redesigned for 1977 to reflect the new Ford LTD II styling. These new models looked com-

You don't get to see too many 1978 F–350 Crew Cab pickups running around today. The reason for that is that most of them were run pretty hard when they were new and discarded when they wore out. Today, these types of pickups aren't that popular for restoring.

pletely different from the Rancheros they replaced, from the front all the way to the back. On the front side their fenders now came to a point and framed a set-back fiberglass header panel that consisted of a rectangular egg-crate grille flanked by a set of stacked headlights. The hood was redesigned, as were the doors and the rear quarter panels. This new look would hold fast for the Ranchero until the last one was produced at the end of the 1979 model year.

Following in the Ranchero's footsteps, Ford's Courier minipickup sported a new look halfway through the model year. Until this point, except for some grille changes, the Courier had used the same body style as it made its debut with back in 1972. The 1977½ Courier, on the other hand, looked quite different from the earlier models. Dissimilarities could be seen in the revamped front fenders, doors, hood and pickup box design. These pickup bodies were now available in short- or long-wheelbase form. Also seeing changes on these trucks were the grille, bumpers, headlights and taillights.

Some thought this restyling of the Courier made it look like a miniaturized F Series pickup, which wasn't a bad deal because the family resemblance probably helped Ford to sell more of them. For those who wanted a deluxe minipickup Ford offered the Courier XLT Appearance Package, which really dressed up this miniworkhorse. A Free Wheeling package was also available for the

Although the Ranger F-150 in this promotional postcard is over ten years old it still looks similar to the Ford F Series trucks sold today. That is staying power.

If you wanted a fancy Ford van in 1979 you could order an Econoline van or Club Wagon with the Captain's Chairs option. This particular option included four Captain's Chairs, full carpeting, a fold-up game table and a combination rear seat/bed arrangement. *Ford Motor Company*

Although not meant as a commercial vehicle, this 1979 Pinto Cruising Van with its flashy graphics would have made for an eye-catching delivery vehicle. *Ford Motor Company*

Courier; it consisted of some tape stripes, fancy wheels and other goodies to help personalize this little truck.

The Bronco soldiered on for one more model year with only minor changes. For those who wanted a sportier appearance on their Broncos Ford offered a Sport Bronco Package, which included chrome bumpers, an argent painted grille, brightmetal headlight and taillight trim, vinyl door panels with dress-up pieces, brightmetal windshield trim and other dress-up goodies. For those who wanted a more deluxe looking Bronco Ford offered the Ranger Package, which consisted of bodyside striping, a swing-away spare tire carrier with spare tire cover, cloth-and-vinyl seat trim, color-keyed carpeting, a color-keyed padded instrument panel, and color-keyed door and side panels.

As far as vanning went in 1977, the models offered in the Econoline and club wagon series were mostly the same as what was offered before. Since these vehicles were so popular, Ford took an "if it isn't broken, don't fix it approach" to them.

Only two changes of note were seen on the F Series line of trucks this year. The first change concerned powerplant choices. The Ford FE Series of big-block engines that had served the Ford car and truck lines so well for so long was now gone. Ford replaced the 360 ci and 390 ci V-8s with truck versions of the 351 ci and 400 ci engines. The 460 ci still was available as an option for buyers of F–150s, F–250s and F–350s, who needed the extra grunt this engine provided.

The other change involved four-wheel-drive versions of the F–250 and F–350 pickups. The early models produced up to midyear were referred to as the high-silhouette models owing to their high cab-to-ground clearance, which made entry and exit difficult, especially for short people. To remedy the situation Ford came out with a revamped low-profile chassis package at midyear, which lowered the cab-step-to-ground clearance by quite a wide margin. When side-by-side comparisons are made, the difference in height between these two trucks is quite evident.

During the 1977 model year the Ford Truck Division reached two milestones that were worthy of celebrations. The first milestone celebrated Ford's sixtieth anni-

Ford made a number of improvements to both their Bronco and F Series truck lines in 1980. *Ford Motor Company*

In 1982 Ford Motorsport offered a set of collectible postcards like this one here for $2. The vehicle pictured is a stock F-150 that was driven to and from and competed in that year's Baja 1000 Off Road Race.

versary of truck production, which was started back in 1917 with the Model TTs.

Of even greater magnitude was milestone number two which was celebrated at the end of the sales year when it was learned that the F Series Ford trucks were America's number-one selling vehicles for this model year. This was the first time ever that a truck had received such an honor, and the distinction would be repeated several more times over the next decade and more.

The chief reason for this phenomenon probably had something to do with the recreational vehicle boom that was going on at this time. A lot of buyers were looking at light-duty trucks in a different light and were buying trucks instead of cars to serve as secondary vehicles—or as primary vehicles in some cases.

No matter how you look at it the 1977 model year was a great one for Ford—the model year that made Ford number 1.

Chapter 11

1978-1991 America's Trucks

★★★★	1978-1983 F-100 Styleside pickup
★★★	1978-1983 F-100 Flareside pickup
★★★★	1978-1991 F-150 Styleside pickup
★★★	1978-1991 F-150 Flareside pickup
★★★	1978-1991 F Series Supercab/Crewcab
★★★★	1978-1991 F Series 4x4 pickup
★★★★	1978-1991 F-250 pickup/ stake
★★★	1978-1991 F-350 pickup/ stake
★★	1978-1991 Chassis cab, chassis cowl
★★★	1978-1982 Courier pickup
★★★★	1978-1991 Bronco
★★★★★★	1978-1979 Ranchero
★★★	1978-1991 Econoline van
★★★	1978-1991 Club Wagon
★★★	1978-1982 Econoline Cruisin'/Free Wheeling van
★★★★	1979 F-100 Ranger XLT Indy 500 pickup
★★★	1978 Pinto Cruising Van
★★★	1983-1991 Ranger pickup
★★★★	1983-1991 Ranger 4x4 pickup
★★★	1984-1990 Bronco II
★★★	1984-1990 Eddie Bauer Bronco II
★★★★★★	1985-1991 Eddie Bauer Bronco
★★	1986-1991 Aerostar
★★★★	1991 Explorer

The Bronco grew up in 1978, in more ways than one. The completely restyled version was longer, wider, taller and a lot heavier, as the 1977-1978 Bronco specifications chart shows.

1977-1978 Bronco specifications

Dimension	1977	1978
Wheelbase	92 in.	104 in.
Overall length	152.1 in.	180.3 in.
Overall width	69.1 in.	79.3 in.
Height	70.1 in.	75.5 in.
Weight	3,490 lb	4,509 lb

This new version of the Bronco featured a front-end treatment that was similar in design to that of the F Series line. A removable fiberglass panel covered the rear area and was available in a white or black color. Standard equipment included a 351 ci V-8 and a four-speed manual transmission. Other standard equipment included deep foam-padded bucket seats in a color-keyed interior, brightmetal-finished hubcaps and exterior mirrors, power brakes and, of course, four-wheel-drive. The Bronco buyer also could choose from a wide variety of optional equipment to suit his or her needs.

Besides the base-model Bronco a super-deluxe model was offered too, called the Bronco Ranger XLT.

Apparently this new Bronco appealed to a much wider audience than the first Bronco ever did, as evidenced by its first-year sales numbers. In 1977 a total 13,300 Broncos were produced; in 1978 that number jumped to over 70,500 vehicles. Ford had every right to be proud of this performance and proud that its new Bronco was an overnight success.

The Econolines and Couriers, except for minor trim changes, stayed pretty much the same as what was offered in 1977. The F Series line of trucks sported a new front-end design that encompassed a larger grille

Bronco XLT models in a two-tone finish like the one shown on this promotional postcard add a touch of class to the four-wheel-drive utility market.

1979–1983

Ford went into the 1979 model year with the same line-up it had in 1978. No changes were in store for the Bronco, but the Econoline received a new grille. For the Courier a 2 liter four-cylinder powerplant became the base engine, and backing it up was a new four-speed transmission. Automatic or five-speed transmissions were available at an extra cost.

The F Series trucks got rectangular headlights across the board, but other than that change everything stayed pretty much the same.

This was the Ranchero's swan song year because after 1979 it was no longer offered by the Ford Motor Company. Once again the Ranchero was available as three separate models—the Ranchero 500, Ranchero GT and Ranchero Squire. Of the three models the GT was the most popular, with sales totaling more than 12,000 units. Total Ranchero sales this year amounted to a little more than 25,000 units.

In May of 1979 the Ford Mustang was chosen to be the pace car for the Indianapolis 500 mile race, and Ford celebrated the event by producing about 5,000 Pace Car Replicas in a special Pewter color with black stripes and Indy 500 decals. Ford also provided some trucks to be used as support vehicles at the racetrack during the month of May. These special trucks were also painted in the special scheme that was featured on the Mustangs. And, as it did with the Mustang, Ford offered a Pace Car Truck Package for those who wanted something special in truck form. This package was offered only on the Styleside pickups, but some original actual Indy 500 support vehicles were sold to the public after the race, and you might be lucky enough to find one of these. Ford supplied sixty support trucks, and this fleet was made up of Broncos, Econoline vans, Econoline club wagons, F Series tow trucks and F Series pickups. All were painted in the Indy 500 special colors of Pewter and black.

For 1980 a new aerodynamic front-end treatment was featured on the Broncos and the F Series trucks. Other than this change everything stayed pretty much the same across the board.

For the 1981 model year no changes of note appeared for any of Ford's light-duty trucks.

The year 1982 was the last for the Mazda-built Ford Courier pickup in the United States, for this model was replaced by a homegrown, all-Ford minitruck called the Ranger. This new truck looked more like a scaled-down version of the full-size F Series trucks than like the Courier. Ford called these new trucks, which it introduced at midyear, 1983 models. The Ranger came standard with a 2 liter four-cylinder power-plant, or with optional engines like a 2.2 liter diesel-powered four-cylinder, a 2.3 liter

gasoline-powered four-cylinder and a 2.8 liter V-6.

A new grille gave the Bronco a different look, but the Econoline and the Courier stayed looking the same as they did in 1981.

Like the Bronco, the F Series trucks received a new grille and new "lubed for life" ball joints. The new F Series trucks also featured provisions for adjusting front-end camber.

In the 1983 model year no big changes occurred for any of Ford's light-duty vehicles.

1984–1987

Despite what you may have heard, only one company led the light-duty commercial field of the early nineties. And it had been that way since the early eighties. Time and again the clear-cut leader in the United

The sedan delivery is alive and well down under as this Aussie Van would have us believe. This Falcon derivative can be used for both work and play. *Michael MacSems collection*

The Ford Bantam is a mini pickup that is based on the Escort platform. This pickup is built in South Africa for that market. *Michael MacSems collection*

States was Ford. As a matter of fact, the Ford F Series truck was the number-one selling vehicle in the US market from at least 1984 to 1991. Ford also dominated the van market

Jeff Huber drove this Chief Auto Parts–sponsored Ford Ranger off-road racer in the Mickey Thompson Off-Road Stadium Series in 1984.

with its Econolines, and it was a force to be reckoned with in the minitruck field with the Ranger. And let's not forget the Bronco in the four-wheel-drive utility class.

In the competitive world of truck sales today you don't achieve the goal of leading the pack without knowing your market and giving the customer what they want when they want it. During the eighties the Ford Truck Division was sensitive to the needs of the market and provided vehicles that met those needs.

In 1983, when the personal utility market wanted a slightly smaller, more economical four-wheel-drive unit, Ford responded by bringing the 1984 Bronco II to market. This little beauty was smaller in size than the regular Bronco, but it was just as tough and a lot more manageable. The market responded well to this new Ford, and pretty soon Bronco IIs were appearing on US highways and byways in large numbers.

Ranger XLT pickups in a two-tone finish like this one add a touch of class to these economy vehicles. The model featured on this postcard is a 1984.

Ford F Series Super cab pickups like this 1984 model in the F-250 line offered a commercial vehicle that could take families out into the wilderness in comfort.

Most people liked this new Bronco because of its compact dimensions and the 115 hp that its standard 171 ci V-6 engine put out. They also liked the wide variety of Bronco II models that were available. Choices included the base Bronco II, the luxurious Bronco XLT and the sporty Bronco XLS, and for those who liked a taste of the outdoors with their Bronco IIs the Eddie Bauer model, named after the famous outfitters.

Other than receiving some trim updates the rest of the Ford light-duty commercial line-up stayed pretty much the same as it was during 1983—except for the venerable F-100. In the line-up since 1953 the F-100 was dropped and replaced by the F-150 as Ford's base model truck. The F-150 had always been a heavy-duty version of the F-100 anyway, and when it seemed customers preferred the F-150 over the F-100 Ford saw no reason to continue with the two separate models. Still a little sadness probably was felt in Dearborn the day that decision was made, since the F-100 was a sentimental favorite to a lot of people who worked for the Ford Truck Division. This model had remained steadfast and true through all the good times as well as the bad during the thirty years it was in production.

Though by looking at them you couldn't tell, in 1985 lots of changes were made to the Ford light-duties clear across the board.

Starting at the low end of the scale with the Ranger a new, more powerful 2.3 liter

1979 Official Indy 500 Truck Package

Silver Metallic paint with unique tape striping in black with red and orange accents

Special black painted push bar

10 hole aluminum wheels

L78x15 raised white letter on-off road tires

Low-gloss black paint applied to front bumper

Black headlight housings and grille insert

Grille surround bar painted argent

Tailgate appliqué with black *Ford* letters on an orange field

Spare tire lock (if optional underframe tire carrier was ordered)

Special seat trim with black vinyl bolsters, silver soft vinyl seat trim inserts with red vinyl welt accents

Black rubber floor mats

Black door panels with special silver pleated vinyl trim inserts with red accented brightmoldings

Brightmetal instrument panel moldings with red inserts on left and right side

Black glovebox appliqué

Black headliner and black sun visors

Black painted rear bumper

Regular bodyside moldings (deleted)

Special commemorative Indy 500 decals

Note: The 1979 Official Indy 500 Truck package was available on long-wheelbase F-100 and F-150 Styleside pickups, and some tow trucks, with Ranger trim.

This factory promotional photograph shows a new 1985 Bronco II XLT in a wilderness setting. *Ford Motor Company*

Electronic Fuel Injection (EFI) four-cylinder engine replaced the carbureted version used before. This new fuel delivery system provided for more power as well as better economy, because the computer with all its sensors could better read the needs of the engine over a wide range of situations. The computer was also able to make adjustments to those needs a lot faster than could human input. Optional engines available for the Ranger included a new turbocharged four-cylinder diesel and a 2.8 liter V–6. For shift-less fans a new automatic overdrive four-speed transmission with an electronically controlled torque converter was available at extra cost.

Steel-belted radial tires replaced the fiberglass-belted tires that were standard on the Ranger before, and a longer list of optional equipment allowed a customer to order a unit that was better suited to his or her particular needs. And finally, better rust-proofing techniques on the Ranger and oth-

er Ford trucks built this year helped to make their bodies last longer.

Over in the Bronco II camp some changes seen included the dropping of its four-speed manual transmission as the base transmission and the inclusion of an improved five-speed overdrive unit. As with the Ranger, a 2.3 liter turbocharged diesel engine was offered as an optional powerplant to the standard 2.8 liter V–6.

The Bronco II sported a lot of standard equipment that was previously optional at extra cost—items like a transfer case skid plate, tinted glass and a cigarette lighter. Also standard at no extra charge was a coat of polyurethane—a chip-resistant paint applied to all lower bodyside areas to help combat rusting problems.

The top-of-the-line Bronco II Eddie Bauer now had Privacy Glass, and a tilt steering wheel with integral cruise control buttons, as standard equipment. The XLT now came with an AM/FM stereo radio, a deluxe leather-wrapped steering wheel and new cloth seat covers, at no extra charge. The Bronco II XLS now came with a tilt steering wheel with integral cruise control buttons, and side door vent windows, at no extra charge.

Moving up in size from the small Bronco II to the regular-size Bronco for 1985 Ford improved quite a few things to make these vehicles more appealing.

Like that of other Ford trucks the Bronco's engine line-up now featured EFI systems to offer more power and economy. The four-speed automatic overdrive transmission was available as an option. The new Broncos also received a new front stabilizer bar for better handling characteristics.

On the inside these new Broncos used black control knobs on their instrument panel, and a black polypropylene plastic material replaced the fiberboard material used on the glovebox, improving its appearance. Standard equipment on the regular Bronco included glovebox locks, high-output heaters and interval wipers.

The 1985 Broncos received upgraded wheel and tire combinations, a new lighter-weight aluminum crossflow radiator and better rustproofing. For those who liked luxury the Bronco XLT looked richer with new seat cover trim. And if you wanted an Eddie Bauer version of the regular Bronco you could get one of those too, since that

A 1985 Ranger XLT 4x4 pickup in a two-tone gray finish. Its V-6 engine and four-wheel-drive made driving off road a piece of cake. *Ford Motor Company*

At the start of the 1990 model year the Bronco II made its debut with a new aerodynamic front-end treatment. Production of the Bronco II ended when the Explorer was introduced as a 1991 model in the Spring of 1990. *Ford Motor Company*

option was expanded to include the larger Bronco.

With all these changes on the Bronco and Bronco IIs you might think nothing was left for the F Series trucks, but Ford held a little in reserve for its bread-and-butter truck line. As with the other trucks, EFI and the four-speed automatic overdrive transmission were available in this series too. In addition a new dual wheel option was made available for the F-350. Power steering became standard equipment on all F-150s with two-wheel-drive, and a new model, the XLT Lariat, became the top-of-the-line model in the F Series ranks.

A new star was on the Ford light-duty commercial horizon in 1986. This new star actually made its debut during the 1985 model year as an early model 1986. (These midyear introductions were starting to become standard operating procedure for Ford,

allowing it to get the jump on the competition.) The new model, called the Aerostar, was meant to appeal to the station wagon crowd as well as the typical van buyer. It was a true van or wagon in a new smaller, trimmer package.

The objectives of the Aerostar program were to give Ford a vehicle that got good fuel economy numbers, like those of a small compact car, while handling a payload or a bunch of passengers almost as well as a full-size van would. These new Aerostars could handle up to seven passengers in comfort and showcase all the latest equipment available from Ford.

Though these were good points, the one feature that made the Aerostar stand out from the crowd was its bold, high-tech exterior styling. From its wedge front end to its slippery back side the Aerostar was aerodynamically clean.

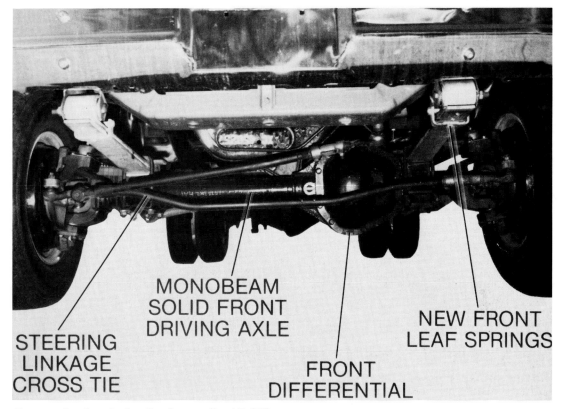

STEERING LINKAGE CROSS TIE

MONOBEAM SOLID FRONT DRIVING AXLE

FRONT DIFFERENTIAL

NEW FRONT LEAF SPRINGS

Front underchassis details of a new Ford F–350 Super Duty 4x4. *Ford Motor Company*

Like its full-size Econoline counterparts the Aerostar was available in van or wagon models in base, XL and XLT trim. The base engine found under its hood was a 2.3 liter EFI four-cylinder unit, with a 2.8 liter V–6 optional. Base transmission was a five-speed manual, with the new four-speed automatic overdrive optional. Other nice features found on the Aerostar included a self-adjusting clutch, manual variable-ratio rack-and-pinion steering on the vans, and power variable-ratio rack-and-pinion steering on the wagons.

Ford made quite a few changes on the Ranger to make it even more appealing to the minitruck market. Now the Ranger line-up consisted of five models. The base model was the Ranger S, which was a regular-cab model on a short wheelbase.

The Ranger model was next on the ladder. This one was available in short or long wheelbase, as a regular-cab model or as a new Super Cab model, and in two- or four-wheel-drive version.

Ranger model number 3 was the Ranger XL, which featured upgraded interior and exterior trim in addition to what was found on Ranger models.

Ranger model number 4, the Ranger XLT, was the top-of-the-line model found on the new Super Cabs.

The fifth choice was the STX Ranger, a sporty version that had black exterior accents, a luxury cloth interior with bucket seats, a leather-wrapped steering wheel, a tachometer and a new 2.9 liter EFI V–6 engine.

Other Ranger highlights included a new "shift on the fly" four-wheel-drive system that could be engaged while the vehicle was moving. Power steering became standard equipment on Ranger 4x4 models, as did a skid plate to protect the transfer case.

The big news for Bronco II fans in 1986 was the availability, for the first time, of a two-wheel-drive version of this popular four-wheel-drive vehicle. The new Bronco II 4x4s also were available with "shift on the fly" four-wheel-drive if a customer desired. Other new features on the Bronco II were a 71 amp-hr battery, single door and ignition keys, low-engine-oil light on the dash and the new 2.9 liter EFI V–6 engine.

The rest of the 1986 Ford light-duty truck line stayed virtually the same as before.

Aerodynamics played a starring role in the looks that were found on the 1987 F Series Ford trucks, as well as the full-size Bronco. To make these vehicles cut through the air in a slippier fashion Ford equipped them with a new front-end treatment with wrap-around halogen headlamps and an airfoil-styled front bumper. These trucks also featured modified fenders, a different grille and redesigned fender wheelwells. They also sat a little lower than what was offered before, to help cut down on wind resistance.

On the inside these redesigned trucks got a new instrument cluster developed specifically for the driver with a full complement of gauges. Under the hood the standard 300 ci six now was equipped with EFI for better fuel economy, power and a better torque curve.

The Twin I-Beam front axle was modified on these trucks so that caster and camber adjustments could be made. The ride was improved by adding gas-pressurized shocks and by employing a recalibrated set of springs on the back side.

As a new safety feature, the new F Series trucks, as well as both Broncos in 1987, were fitted with a new rear-wheel antilockup braking system (ABS). This system helped to control the back end during panic stops.

Super Duty F-350 models offered the toughness of a medium-duty truck in a light-duty truck package. This model is equipped with four-wheel-drive, four-wheel disk brakes and dual rear wheels. *Ford Motor Company*

A Saleen-prepped Ranger race truck that competed in the SCCA Coors Race Truck Challenge Series.

Aerostar Equipment
Power brakes (disc front, drum rear)
17 gallon fuel tank
Halogen headlamps
One-piece rear liftgate
P185/75R 14SL steel-belted radial tires
14x5 in. wheels (van)
14x5.5 in. wheels (wagon)
Flush-mounted glass
Color-coordinated front and rear plastic bumpers
Tinted glass (wagons)
Black plastic front spoiler
Argent painted styled steel wheels (van)
Brushed stainless steel wheel covers (wagon)
Inside hood release
Vinyl seat covers
Backlit instrument cluster and lighted speedometer needle
Full carpeting (wagons)
Carpeted front floor (van)
Specifications: 118.9 in. wheelbase
   174.9 in. overall length

72.8 in. overall height
71.7 in. overall width
61.5 in. front tread
60.0 in. rear tread
143.2 cu ft cargo space (van)
175.9 cu ft cargo space when right front seat removed (van)
1,200 lb standard payload rating (van)
2,000 lb maximum payload rating (van)

1985 Bronco Eddie Bauer Equipment
5.0 liter EFI engine
Tilt steering wheel with cruise controls
Air conditioning
Raised white letter all-terrain tires
Deluxe styled steel wheels
Unique two-tone: Light Desert Tan rear cap and matching tan lower bodyside paint with the choice of 3 primary bodyside colors
XLT-level tan interior with captain's chairs and exclusive Eddie Bauer cloth trim
Extended care service plan
Eddie Bauer gear bag and map folder

The 1989 Ford Ranger. The engine featured two spark plugs per cylinder. This arrangement helped to boost power and economy, as well as producing cleaner emissions. *Ford Motor Company*

1988–1990

For the 1988 model year Ford's major emphasis centered around a program to provide better rustproofing properties in its F Series line. Galvanized steel was now used for inner and outer hood panels, front floor pans, roof panels, rear corner panels, running boards, inner and outer door panels, and outer cowl side panels. These galvanized panels and a change in Ford's painting practices helped these trucks, and those that followed, to better deal with the ravages of rust.

Ford also made news during the model year by releasing a new line of Super Duty F-350s with GVW ratings of 14,500 lb. These new models based in the light-duty line featured all sorts of big truck parts to give them a tougher edge—parts like an 11,000 lb. rated monobeam front axle, tapered front leaf springs, four-wheel-disc brakes, longer wheelbases, 16 in. wheels, dual rear wheels, and the choice of a 7.5 liter gasoline engine or a torquey 7.3 liter diesel.

For the 1989 model year most of Ford's truck development budget went into revising the Ranger and Bronco II models to make them look and perform in a more contemporary fashion.

Both the Ranger and the Bronco IIs featured new aerodynamic front-end treatments that consisted of rectangular wraparound halogen headlights with integral turn signal lamps. They also featured restyled front fenders, bumpers and a restyled grille.

Under the hood the new Rangers carried a more powerful standard four-cylinder engine. The power increase came from a new head design with twin spark plugs for each cylinder, revised intake ports and combustion chambers. A new redesigned intake

manifold and distributorless ignition systems were also found on this engine.

The new Rangers were also fitted with a rear ABS and revalved shock absorbers. Inside changes included a column-mounted automatic transmission shift lever and a new instrument cluster.

The Bronco II featured most of the same changes found on the Ranger and some of its own too. For example it had richer-looking interiors and more exterior color choices.

For the F Series truck the E40D automatic overdrive four-speed transmission was made an option with heavy-duty pickups and heavy-duty Econolines. And extended-length models were added to the Aerostar line-up for those who needed a little extra room.

Highlights for the 1990 model year included the addition of a new more powerful

The new Ford Explorer has proven to be a winner for the Ford Motor Company. Although it's only been out for a short period of time it is setting new sales records and receiving praise from the media and the public alike. *Ford Motor Company*

4.0 liter V-6 engine producing 160 hp at 240 lb-ft of torque as an option for the Ranger, the Bronco II and the Aerostars. Rear antilock brakes made an appearance on the Aerostar and Econolines, and automatic locking hubs became standard equipment on the F-150 4x4 pickups. The E40D automatic overdrive four-speed transmission availability was extended to include all F Series trucks and all Econolines too. And a new electronically controlled four-wheel-drive system was offered as optional equipment to Aerostar customers. This system was fully automatic, requiring no driver input at all. It engaged itself whenever sensors placed at each wheel indicated the need for extra traction.

1991

The big news this year came about in the spring when Ford once again released an early 1991 model called the Explorer. This new utility vehicle was meant to replace the Bronco II. Like the Bronco II it could be had in two- and four-wheel-drive form, but unlike the Bronco II it was available in two- or four-door form. The four-door version was the most popular, outselling the two-door by more than a 9.5:1 margin.

The Explorer featured all-new styling front to rear and utilized the 4.0 liter EFI V-6 engine. Transmission choices included a standard five-speed manual or the optional E40D automatic overdrive. This new model also came equipped with a rear ABS, "shift on the fly" four-wheel-drive, gas-pressurized shocks, stabilizer bars front and rear, large P225 metric radial tires and a rear step bumper. The Ford Explorer was also the first Ford truck in which the JBL Audio System was offered as optional equipment.

Parts Sources

Many parts that are needed to restore Ford trucks are still available at your local Ford dealer. However, if you can't find what you need there you might want to contact one of the following sources:

Arizona

Arizona F-100 Parts
5230 W. Lake #2
Glendale, AZ 85301
    New, new-old-stock (NOS), used and reproduction parts.

Jim Dottling
728 E. Dunlap
Phoenix, AZ 85020
    Falcon parts; catalog available.

Don Sanderson Ford
Specialty Parts Division
5300 Grand Ave.
Glendale, AZ 85301
    1953-1956 F-100 parts.

California

Clifford Research
15572 Computer Lane
Huntington Beach, CA 92649
    High-performance intake and exhaust systems for Ford six-cylinders.

SoCal Pickups
6321 Manchester Blvd.
Buena Park, CA 90621
    1953-1956 Ford pickups.

Sacramento Vintage Ford Parts
1504 El Camino Ave.
Sacramento, CA 95815
    1948-1960 truck parts; catalog available.

Truck Stop
1477 N. Carolan
Burlingame, CA 94010

Valley Ford Parts
11610 Vanowen St.
North Hollywood, CA 91605
    Bronco, Falcon, F Series trucks; NOS parts; catalog available.

Ford Obsolete
9107-13 Garvey Ave.
Rosemead, CA 91770

F-100 Parts Unlimited
18651 Walnut St.
Clements, CA 95227-0250

Concours Parts and Accessories
PO Box 1210
Santa Ynez, CA 93460
    1948-1966 F Series trucks.

Vintage Auto Parts
402 W. Chapman Ave.
Orange, CA 92666
    NOS and reproduction parts.

A C Enterprises
14804 Tulipland
Canyon Country, CA 91351
    New and used parts for 1953–1956
Ford pickups.

All Ford Parts
655 N. 8th St.
San Jose, CA 95112
    1909–1952 Ford trucks.

C&G Early Ford Parts
165 Balboa St., C11
San Marcos, CA 92069
    1932–1956 Ford parts.

Colorado
John's TZ Stuff
740 12th St.
Boulder, CO 80302
    1957–1972 F Series trucks.

Sam's Vintage Ford Parts
5105 Washington
Denver, CO 80216
    1949–1970 parts.

Connecticut
Glasco
69 Industrial Park Rd. E.
Tolland, CT 06084
    Glass products for all trucks.

Georgia
Obsolete Ford Parts
Box 787
Nashville, GA 31639
    1957–1972 parts for F Series, Falcons,
Econolines; catalog available.

Illinois
Merkel Model Car Company
PO Box 689
Franklin Park, IL 60131
    Toy trucks and cars.

Indiana
Old Cars
505 S. Tibbs
Indianapolis, IN 76241
    Parts for F Series, Falcons, Rancheros.

Kansas
Cornelius Ford Parts
3343 N. 61st St.
Kansas City, KS 66104
    1942–1960 NOS and reproduction
parts; catalog available.

Rick's Antique Auto Parts
2754 Roe Lane
Kansas City, KS 66103
    1948–1965 reproduction parts; catalog
available.

Kentucky
King and Wesley Obsolete Parts
Courthouse Sq.
Liberty, KY 42539
    Falcon, Fairlane, and F Series parts.

Bill White
Box 32262-SR2
Louisville, KY 40232
    Shop manuals and other paper
collectibles.

Maryland
Anderson Industries
6599 Washington Blvd.
Elkridge, MD 21227
    Fiberglass body parts.

Massachusetts
Northeast F-100 Parts
62 Wheeler Rd.
Rutland, MA 01543
    1948–1966 F-100 parts; catalog
available.

Michigan
Muscle Parts
PO Box 2579
Dearborn, MI 48123

Minnesota
Little Dearborn Parts
2424 University Ave.
Minneapolis, MN 55414
    NOS and reproduction parts.

Missouri
Mack Products
Box 278
Moberly, MO 65270
    1926-1956 Ford pickup beds.

Nebraska
Mike Dennis
1845 S. 48th
Lincoln, NE 68506
    NOS parts for Falcon and F Series.

Nevada
Bob's Classic Auto Glass
341 A Moran St.
Reno, NV 89502
    Glass products for all Fords.

Fabulous Falcons
5564 Slope Drive
Reno, NV 89431
    Falcon parts.

New Hampshire
Page's Model A Garage
Main St.
Haverhill, NH 03765
    1932-1953 parts.

New Jersey
Last Chance Ford Parts
435 S. Main St.
PO Box 1116
Forked River, NJ 08731
    1932 and later parts.

New York
Joblot Automotive
98-11 211th St.
Queens Village
Long Island, NY 11429
    Mechanical parts for 1948-1964 Ford trucks; catalog available.

Muck Motors Ford
10 Campbell Blvd.
Getzville, NY 14068

North Carolina
Dennis Carpenter
PO Box 26398
Charlotte, NC 28221
    1940-1972 Ford truck parts; catalog available.

Dan Carpenter
Route 2, Box 390AA
Norwood, NC 28128
    Sheet metal parts for Ford truck beds.

Carolina Classics
624 E. Greer St.
Durham, NC 27701
    1948-1966 Ford trucks; catalog available.

Ohio
Green Sales Co.
427 W. Seymour
Cincinnati, OH 45216
    NOS parts for F Series, Falcons, Fairlanes.

Old Ford Parts
Box 148
Englewood, OH 45322
    1939-1970 Ford parts.

Ford Parts Store
4925 Ford Rd., Box 226
Bryan, OH 43506
    1954-1965 parts.

Antique Auto Sheet Metal
718 Albert Rd.
Brookville, OH 45309
    1928-1929 roadster pickup bodies.

Oklahoma
Obsolete Ford Parts
6601 S. Shields
Oklahoma City, OK 73149
    1948-1972 truck parts.

Steve Davis
3909 Cashion Pl.
Oklahoma City, OK 73112
    New and used Ford truck parts.

Oregon

Northwest Classic Falcons
1964 NW Pettygrove
Portland, OR 97209
  Falcon parts.

Jerry Bougher Truck Ads
3628 Union St. SE
Albany, OR 97321
  Truck magazine ads.

Bob Drake Reproductions
1819 NW Washington Blvd.
Grants Pass, OR 97526
  Reproduction rubber parts.

Buds F–100 Parts
945 La Salle St.
Harrisburg, OR 97446
  F–100 parts.

Texas

Don White
801 N. 4th St.
Princeton, TX 75077
  Ranchero parts.

Specialized Auto Parts
7310 Capital, Box 9405
Houston, TX 77261
  1909–1948 parts.

Virginia

Chewnings Auto Literature
123 N. Main St.
Broadway, VA 22815
  Owners manuals.

Auto Krafters
Box 392
Timberville, VA 22853
  F Series, Falcon, Fairlane parts.

Washington

City Motor Company
944 6th St.
Clarkston, WA 99403
  Falcon and Fairlane parts.

West Virginia

Ed Baker
Box 141
Nitro, WV
  NOS Ford truck parts.

Wisconsin

Modine Manufacturing
1500 Dekoven Ave.
Racine, WI 53401
  Radiators.

Canada

Mercury Madness
24898 56th Ave.
Aldergrove, BC
Canada VOX 1A0
  Mercury truck parts.

Clubs

The Early Ford V8 Club of America
PO Box 2122
San Leandro, CA 94577
   1932–1953 Fords.

The Econoline Organization
258 Cambridge St.
San Leandro, CA 94577
   1961–1967 Ford Econolines.

Fabulous Fifties Ford Club of America
PO Box 286
Riverside, CA 92502
   1949–1960 Fords.

Falcon Club of America
PO Box 113
Jacksonville, AR 72076
   All Falcons.

Model A Ford Club of America
250 S. Cypress
La Habra, CA 90631
   All Model A Fords.

Model T Ford Club of America
Box 7400
Burbank, CA 91510
   All Model T Fords.

Model T Ford Club International
PO Box 438315
Chicago, IL 60643
   All Model T Fords.

Model A Restorers Club
24822 Michigan Ave.
Dearborn, MI 48124
   All Model A Fords.

The Ranchero Club
1339 Beverly Rd.
Port Vue, PA 15133
   All Rancheros.

Light Commercial Vehicle Association
c/o Irvin Neubert
Route 14, Box 468
Jonesboro, TN 37659
   All light-duty commercial vehicles.

American Truck Historical Society
PO Box 59200
Birmingham, AL 35259
   All trucks.

Performance Ford Club of America
PO Box 32
Ashville, OH 43103
   All Ford-powered vehicles.

Recommended Reading

If you like reading books that deal with Ford commercial vehicles, you might want to pick up a copy, or copies, of the following titles:

Standard Catalog of American Light-Duty Trucks by John Gunnell. Krause Publications. Covers all light-duty trucks built between 1896 and 1986. This great reference book examines all the well-known makes, as well as the more obscure. It contains over 700 pages of material.

Ford Trucks Since 1905 by James Wagner. Considered to be the major work on this subject because just about every Ford truck model ever produced is covered. Lots of photographs and text make this book a must-read for all serious students of Ford trucks.

Ford Pickup Trucks: Development History and Restoration Guide 1948–56 by Paul G. McLaughlin. Motorbooks International. Covers all Ford light-duty commercial vehicles produced during the 1948–56 period. This book contains lots of photographs, specification sheets and reprinted sales materials.

Ford Pickups 1957–1967 by Paul G. McLaughlin. Motorbooks International. Picks up where McLaughlin's first book stops. This text covers all Ford light-duty commercial vehicles produced during the 1957–67 era. It includes information and photographs on F Series trucks, Couriers, Rancheros, Econolines, Broncos and foreign Fords.

Hemmings Motor News, Box 100, Bennington, VT 05201. Considered the bible of the auto collecting hobby. This periodical has been published for more than thirty-five years.

Thousands of ads appear every month and cover parts, services and vehicles.

Pickup and Van Spotters Guide 1945–1982 by Tad Burness. Motorbooks International. Uses photographs and clippings from original sales materials to provide an easy-to-read, easy-to-use, entertaining book to help identify these vehicles.

Illustrated History of Ford by George Damman. Crestline. Covers Ford vehicles, including some trucks, through the 1970 model year.

The Heavyweight Book of American Light Trucks 1939–1966 by Don Bunn and Tom Brownell. Motorbooks International. Covers all light-duty trucks produced from 1939 through 1966. This good reference book examines all makes and models from the well-known to the not-so-well-known. It contains lots of photographs, plus period advertisements, drawings and text to provide hours of interesting reading.

Truckin' magazine. Covers all aspects of truck information with a slant toward modifications. This magazine features articles on both new and old vehicles. It is available at most newsstands.

The Ford Y-Block: Origin, Maintenance, Rebuild by James Eickman. Motorbooks International. Offers a complete guide to the Ford Y-block V-8 engines that were installed in Ford cars and trucks from 1954 through 1964.

Classic Motorbooks Ford Ranchero 1957–1979 Photofacts by Bill Siuru and Bill Holder. Motorbooks International. Uses lots of photographs and text to cover Ford Rancheros from their start to their finish.